6+7,
67-82

218+19
222--25
227
231-3

LABOR RELATIONS AND PUBLIC POLICY SERIES

NO. 20

THE IMPACT OF THE AT&T-EEO CONSENT DECREE

by

HERBERT R. NORTHRUP

and

JOHN A. LARSON

INDUSTRIAL RESEARCH UNIT
The Wharton School, Vance Hall/CS
University of Pennsylvania
Philadelphia, Pennsylvania 19104
U.S.A.

5924896

Foreword

In 1968, the Industrial Research Unit inaugurated its Labor Relations and Public Policy Series as a means of examining issues and stimulating discussions in the complex and controversial areas of collective bargaining and the regulation of labor-management disputes. This study, *The Impact of the AT&T-EEO Consent Decree*, is the twentieth monograph published in the series. Eleven of these studies deal with various aspects of National Labor Relations Board procedures and policies. The other nine, including this one, explain significant and controversial issues such as welfare and strikes; opening the skilled construction trades to blacks; the Davis-Bacon Act; the labor-management situation in urban school systems; old age, handicapped, and Vietnam-era antidiscrimination legislation; and the impact of the Occupational Safety and Health Act. All of these studies are concerned with explaining the effects, financial and otherwise, of government regulatory measures on the ability of corporate management to carry out its function of operating enterprises.

The consent decree entered into in 1973 between the world's largest private company, the American Telephone and Telegraph Company, and several government agencies, particularly the Equal Employment Opportunity Commission, the U.S. Department of Labor, and the U.S. Department of Justice, for the purpose of increasing the participation of minorities and women in AT&T jobs was a landmark in the field of equal employment. Large amounts of back pay were paid to women and minorities, and goals were set which, as interpreted, had to be met for the company to stay in compliance. Thus, we have a five-year program, ended in January 1979, which provided for a quota system of employment throughout the Bell Telephone system.

Despite much that has been written about the consent decree, no one has undertaken to determine what happened. What proportion of blacks, other minorities, and women received jobs as a result? What has been the impact on the management and operation of the system? What else can we learn from this unique experience?

The Industrial Research Unit was anxious to fill this void. Originally, an approach was made to the entire utility industry to update the book *Negro Employment in Public Utilities*, which the

iii

Industrial Research Unit published in 1970 as part of the Studies of Negro Employment series. After some negotiations, the electric and gas utilities declined to participate, but the Bell System enthusiastically endorsed the idea and contributed a small grant to get the study under way. The bulk of the funding came from the Industrial Research Unit's unrestricted funds provided largely by the eighty-five companies that are members of its American Research Advisory Group and from unrestricted grants in support of the Labor Relations and Public Policy Series by the J. Howard Pew Freedom Trust and the John M. Olin Foundation.

The Bell System's role in this study was to provide the information and to make its officials available for interviews. System officials were interviewed at headquarters and operating personnel in all areas of the country by the authors who did all the interviewing. Data were supplied from the central headquarters, which has most of the information on tape and in excellent form for analysis.

The coauthor of this monograph, John A. Larson, is a graduate of Holy Cross College and earned a Master of Arts degree in economics from the University of Wisconsin before enlisting in the United States Navy, in which he served as an officer for six years. In addition to active duty, he also served as an instructor at the Naval Postgraduate School and remained there as an adjunct professor in a civilian capacity for a short period upon completion of his military service. In May 1979, he was awarded the Master of Business Administration degree from the graduate division of the University of Pennsylvania's Wharton School.

Many persons assisted in this work. Special mention should be made of Dr. H. Weston Clarke, Jr., Vice-President, Human Resources, AT&T, who was interested in the project from the first and provided necessary clearances and support on which the study depended. He was ably assisted in this respect by John A. Kingsbury, Assistant Vice-President; D. E. Liebers, Director— Equal Opportunity and Affirmative Action; Donald D. Morgan, Staff Specialist; and Raj Natarajan, Personnel Support Analyst. We also wish to thank the many operating executives throughout the system who spent considerable time in discussing these matters with us, as did Lee H. White, Assistant for Public Relations, Communication Workers of America, and John W. Shaughnessy, President, Telecommunications International Union. David A. Copus, Esquire, who was the chief negotiator for the Equal Employment Opportunity Commission and, in a real sense, the intellectual father of the decree, and who is now in private practice, was also most helpful.

The manuscript was typed by our secretarial staff, Nancy E. Chiang, Carolyn W. Free, Kathryn Hunter, and Judith A. Pepper. It was edited by Donna Fex, Assistant Editor of the Industrial Research Unit, and the index was done by Joyce Post. Margaret E. Doyle, Office Manager, handled the necessary administrative tasks with her usual efficiency.

The views expressed, of course, are solely the authors' and should not be attributed to anyone in the American Telephone and Telegraph Company and its operating companies, to the grantors, or to the University of Pennsylvania.

Herbert R. Northrup, *Director*
Industrial Research Unit
The Wharton School
University of Pennsylvania

Philadelphia
July 1979

TABLE OF CONTENTS

LIST OF TABLES

TABLE   PAGE

TABLE   PAGE

TABLE   PAGE

LIST OF FIGURES

FIGURE

CHAPTER I

Development of the Decree

The consent decree agreed to in January 1973 by the American Telephone and Telegraph Company (AT&T) and the United States Equal Employment Opportunity Commission (EEOC), the Department of Justice, and the Department of Labor was a milestone of EEOC enforcement. The largest company in America was to change its employment policies, to pay money damages to classes allegedly aggrieved, and to meet various employment targets for women and minorities. The signing of the decree marked a new stage in EEO enforcement and induced the EEOC and other governmental agencies in the equal employment field not only to adopt a more aggressive attitude but also to seek punitive money damages as a regular course of action.

In this chapter, we summarize developments leading up to the decree and explain the decree's terms; following chapters analyze the results over the five-year life of the decree.

BACKGROUND

The initiation of changes in December 1970, and the commencement of what was to become a landmark case in the field of equal employment opportunity, was not the first encounter between AT&T and the EEOC. Prior to December 1970, over two thousand cases had been filed with the EEOC charging employment discrimination by individuals protected under the Civil Rights Act of 1964. The EEOC had conducted analyses of several Bell operating companies as well as extensive studies of the entire Bell System. These studies were used as background material for discussions held from 1967 to 1969 between top officials of the EEOC and senior management of AT&T. The negotiations resulted in a commitment by AT&T to pursue a more aggressive policy for hiring and for providing upward mobility for minority employees. AT&T recognized the seriousness and magnitude of the equal employment issue, and by the late 1960s, it was actively pursuing a strategy to improve minority hiring and upgrading. Its efforts in the area of eliminating

1

previous discrimination based upon sex, however, were not as clearly identified or as actively pursued.

AT&T, in accordance with procedures established by the Office of Federal Contract Compliance (OFCC) of the United States Department of Labor,[1] was already submitting data on employment practices and developing guidelines to insure equal employment opportunity. By comparison to many other companies during this period, AT&T was very progressive in its employment practices.

Role of David A. Copus

The igniting force behind the case was a young lawyer named David A. Copus, who then was an attorney on the staff of the EEOC's General Counsel. During 1969 and 1970, Copus was assigned to assist the Public Service Commission of the District of Columbia in a case involving a request for a rate increase by the Potomac Electric Power Company (PEPCO). The Washington, D.C., chapter of the National Urban League was challenging the PEPCO rate increase and moving to have the Public Service Commission deny the increase because of alleged discrimination against minorities by PEPCO. The Public Service Commission petitioned the EEOC for assistance concerning its authority to regulate the employment practices of a public utility under its jurisdiction. Copus was assigned by William H. Brown III, then chairman of the EEOC, to work with the Public Service Commission on this matter.

Under the wording of Title VII of the Civil Rights Act of 1964 (prior to its amendment in 1972), the EEOC was not granted the authority to litigate cases on behalf of the aggrieved party but could enter the case as an *amicus curiae*. Therefore, when PEPCO challenged the authority of the Public Service Commission to impose an affirmative action plan on the company, the EEOC joined as an *amicus*. The proceedings continued into 1971, and the court found that the Public Service Commission did, in fact, have the authority to review PEPCO's employment practices but, for procedural reasons, did not uphold the affirmative action plan as proposed.[2]

It was during the PEPCO litigation that Copus became aware of the rate increase that AT&T was seeking from the Federal Com-

---

[1] The OFCC is now the OFCCP (Office of Federal Contract Compliance Programs). The OFCCP monitors EEO programs of federal contractors and, as a matter of policy, attempts to push companies beyond equal employment with "affirmative action."

[2] *Potomac Electric Power Company v. Public Service Commission of the District of Columbia*, U.S. District Court for the District of Columbia, Civil Action Nos. 2382-70 and 2384-70, February 23, 1971.

munications Commission (FCC). The increase was to apply to federally regulated long-distance telephone service which was under the jurisdiction of the FCC. The relationship was not unlike the relationship between PEPCO and the Public Service Commission. Because of the great number of cases currently pending before the EEOC that involved AT&T (approximately 5 to 6 percent of its total backlog) and the similarity with the PEPCO case, Copus pursued the possibility of the EEOC approaching the FCC with a petition similar to that used by the National Urban League in the PEPCO case. He presented the idea to Chairman William H. Brown III, who approved it and assigned two additional attorneys, Susan Ross and Lawrence Gartner, to assist Copus with the case.

Role of the FCC

On December 10, 1970, the EEOC filed a petition with the FCC opposing the rate increase for AT&T on the grounds of its alleged discriminatory employment practices. Here, again, it must be remembered that the EEOC was unable to litigate the matter itself and could only intervene in the FCC proceeding as a representative of the public interest. The EEOC based its charge upon previously compiled studies and analyses of employment practices within the Bell System and the current backlog of cases entered with the EEOC charging various Bell System operating companies as well as the parent AT&T.

AT&T's petition for a rate increase in long distance telephone service was filed with the FCC on November 19, 1970. It requested that the guaranteed rate of return for the Bell System be increased from 7.5 percent to 9.5 percent.[3] The EEOC petition to intervene in the case was filed on December 10, 1970, and stated:

> That because AT&T's operating companies engage in pervasive and unlawful discrimination in employment against women, blacks, Spanish-surnamed Americans, and other minorities, the rate increase proposed and filed by AT&T with the Commission is unjust and unreasonable, in violation of [the Federal Communications Act of 1934, Title VII of the Civil Rights Act of 1964, the Equal Pay Act of 1963, Executive Order 11246, the Civil Rights Act of 1866, the fair employment practice acts of approximately 30 states and ordinances of numerous large cities]. . . .
>
> Wherefore, petitioner, EEOC asks that the Commission grant the EEOC's Petition to Intervene, suspend the operation of AT&T's proposed rate increase, conduct a hearing, and declare the proposed increase illegal until AT&T's operating companies have ceased their

---

[3] AT&T's petition was docketed as Tariff FCC No. 263.

unlawful discrimination against women, blacks, Spanish-surnamed Americans, and other minorities.[4]

The FCC denied the EEOC's request to intervene in the AT&T rate case based upon alleged employment discrimination. The FCC did, however, rule that the employment practices of AT&T and the Bell System operating companies be investigated in a separate proceeding. On January 21, 1971, the FCC established a separate case, FCC Docket No. 19143, to handle the question of AT&T employment practices.

Another important element of the proceedings with the FCC was the involvement of several civil rights groups that joined the EEOC as copetitioners in the FCC rate case: the National Association for the Advancement of Colored People, the National Organization for Women, the Legal Defense and Education Fund, the American Civil Liberties Union, the California Rural Legal Assistance, the Mexican-American Legal Defense Fund, and the American G.I. Forum. When the FCC ruled to have separate proceedings for investigating AT&T's employment practices, these groups appealed the decision in proceedings that continued into 1974 (after the consent decree had already been signed). Because of this appeal and the possibility of the rate increase being reversed, AT&T was faced with the extra expense and operating problems involved in keeping two sets of accounts—one at the old rates and another at the revised rates.

The role of the FCC in the case is also critical because it provided the EEOC with the opportunity to pursue the charges that it had made against AT&T. The FCC had assumed the responsibility to enforce equal employment opportunity legislation as part of its regulatory efforts and to consult with the EEOC on such matters by recognizing the EEOC in an separate proceeding against AT&T. This gave the EEOC much greater leverage than it would have had in numerous separate cases against the individual operating companies of the Bell System.

FCC Case

The hearings, as provided for by the FCC, were to be initiated in early 1971 to investigate the employment practices of AT&T. The FCC order providing for the hearings identified five general areas of inquiry:

---

[4] Petition for Intervention, Before the FCC, Washington, D.C., Docket No. 19129, *Equal Employment Opportunity Commission v. American Telephone and Telegraph Company,* December 10, 1970, pp. 2–3.

1. Whether the existing employment practices of AT&T tend to impede equal equal employment opportunities in AT&T and its operating companies contrary to other purposes and requirements of the Commission's Rules and the Civil Rights Act of 1964.
2. Whether AT&T has failed to inaugurate and maintain specific programs, pursuant to Commission Rules and Regulations, insuring against discriminatory practices in the recruiting, selection, hiring, placement, and promotion of its employees.
3. Whether AT&T has engaged in pervasive, system-wide discrimination against women, Negroes, Spanish-surnamed Americans, and other minorities in its employment practices.
4. Whether any of the employment practices of AT&T, if found to be discriminatory, affect the rates charged by that company for its services, and if so, in what way is this reflected in the present rate structure.
5. To determine, in light of the evidence adduced pursuant to the foregoing issues, what order, or requirements, if any, should be adopted by the Committee.[5]

The procedure involved in a government hearing such as this begins with the assignment of an administrative law judge and the filing of pretrial briefs by the parties involved, giving their interpretation of the legal issues. Then each party investigates or attempts to "discover" the facts from the other party. This can be done formally or informally and is often a breakdown point in the progression of the hearings. Third, each party presents expert witnesses and testimony on behalf of its position. These witnesses are then cross-examined. In the fourth phase, the parties move to enter various exhibits, documents, and data for the record. These are often challenged, and the administrative law judge has final control over what is admitted and rejected. The fifth and sixth steps involve the submission of proposed finding of facts based upon the record and conclusions of law; after this is completed, the administrative law judge passes judgment on the facts, the law, and the law as applied to the facts. The decision may then be appealed, after which a final administrative decision is made on the case by the presiding authority of the agency involved.[6] Appeal is then provided through the federal courts. It should be noted that AT&T and the government were able to come to an agreement through private negotiations when the hearings had reached only the fourth step. This was approximately two years after the proceedings began.

In April 1971, the EEOC established a special AT&T task force

---

[5] FCC, *Memorandum Opinion and Order,* Docket No. 19143, January 21, 1971, p. 5.
[6] Phyllis A. Wallace and Jack E. Nelson, "Legal Processes and Strategies of Intervention," in *Equal Employment Opportunity and the AT&T Case,* ed. Phyllis A. Wallace (Cambridge, Mass.: MIT Press, 1976), pp. 243–52.

headed by Copus. This group also received substantial support from several university professors specializing in the social sciences. The AT&T team was headed up by George Ashley and Harold Levy, both attorneys for the Bell System. Thompson Powers of Steptoe and Johnson, a Washington law firm, served as counsel for AT&T. John Kingsbury, assistant vice-president for personnel at AT&T, also played an active role in the proceedings.

The preliminary position of the EEOC's task force centered on two major points: (1) employment practices that have a disparate effect on minorities and women and that cannot be defended on grounds of business necessity and (2) practices that perpetuate the effect of past discriminatory conditions, regardless of whether the previous act of discrimination occurred before the passage of the Civil Rights Act of 1964.[7]

AT&T's position, developed in response to the EEOC's prehearing memorandum setting forth the above points for determination as well as the interpretation of the applicable law, was that the EEOC's proposals went beyond the scope of current law and that the Bell System was making a good-faith effort to comply with the current law as AT&T interpreted it.

Although these initial positions were taken and the procedure of the hearings initiated in the spring of 1971, by August of that year, the EEOC and AT&T had entered into private negotiating sessions in hopes of achieving an out-of-court settlement. The informal sessions continued on a weekly basis during the course of the formal proceedings and eventually led to an early settlement.

EEOC Position

The position of the EEOC on the AT&T case was summarized in the report *"A Unique Competence": A Study of Equal Employment Opportunity in the Bell System.* The report made the following points about discrimination against women:

1. Sex segregation was extensive—almost every low-paying job in the Bell System was a "female" job.
2. Males were excluded from "female" jobs and females excluded from "male" jobs on a consistent basis regardless of whether bona fide occupational qualifications could account for the segregation.
3. The Bell System's recruiting, hiring, and promotion practices restricted opportunities for women through various institutional and organizational structures.

---

[7] *Ibid.*

4. Sex-stereotyping of jobs and departments inhibited equal opportunity between the sexes for promotion to better-paying positions.
5. Even if women did receive promotions, their wages were lower than the equivalent male based upon their lower previous wage.[8]

Regarding discrimination against blacks and Hispanics, the report found the following:

1. Most blacks in the Bell System were female and therefore suffered a dual handicap.
2. Black males were highly restricted from the craft jobs and held only the bottom jobs in this category.
3. Very few blacks (2.8 percent) held management jobs in the Bell System.
4. Hispanics were seriously underrepresented in those areas having a significant Hispanic population.
5. Minority employees tended to hold the lowest-paying jobs in the Bell System.[9]

AT&T Position

AT&T summarized its position in a memorandum, *The Bell Companies as Equal Employers: A Record of Achievement, A Commitment to Progress,* which accompanied the testimony of John Kingsbury, AT&T's lead witness, in addition to other plans and documents developed by a special task force of company managers. Kingsbury in his testimony agreed that the Bell System and all other American companies should attempt to eliminate discrimination from their employment policies and that they all had much progress to make in this regard. He disagreed, however, with the EEOC's charge of past discrimination and with the use of current-day standards to measure past discrimination. He also denied the EEOC charge that AT&T discriminated against qualified applicants and asserted the prerogative of the company to establish employment standards for maintaining the quality of its work force. In addition, Kingsbury emphasized the high-skill, high-technology nature of the communications industry and the shortage of female and minority applicants with the necessary technical training to handle effectively many of the positions within the Bell System. He basically stated that the Bell System is not the employer of last resort.

---

[8] *Ibid.*

[9] Phyllis A. Wallace, "Equal Employment Opportunity," in *Equal Employment Opportunity,* pp. 257–68.

In his testimony, Kingsbury also cited past efforts and achievements of the Bell System toward attaining equal employment opportunities and examples of affirmative action:

1. Involvement of AT&T with the National Alliance of Businessmen's JOBS (Job Opportunities in the Business Sector) program to increase employment opportunities for minorities and the disadvantaged.
2. Development of programs to recruit minorities and participation in work-study arrangements.
3. Establishment of a task force to investigate the utilization of women in management.
4. Ongoing compliance reviews of personnel practices.
5. Development of special programs to improve the utilization of Spanish-surnamed Americans.
6. Development of "Early Identification" of potential to accelerate promotions of qualified women and minorities.
7. Job enrichment programs to improve Bell System jobs.[10]

Kingsbury also presented a model affirmative action program, much of which was included in the final agreement with the EEOC. This provided for hiring and promotion targets based upon the statistical breakdown of the relevant labor pool.

In addition to Kingsbury, several expert witnesses also testified for AT&T, including Dr. Hugh Folk, professor of economics at the University of Illinois, who regarded the statistical evidence of the EEOC as being biased and challenged the assumptions about labor market supply and demand relationships.

GSA and DOL

While this testimony was taking place, AT&T was developing its affirmative action plan in an effort to receive approval from the General Services Administration (GSA), the agency charged with overseeing AT&T's "conduct compliance" under the regulations establishing the OFCC.

The remaining key factor in the case is the U.S. Department of Labor. In December 1971, the OFCC issued Revised Order No. 4 requiring affirmative action plans to specify goals and timetables. As a result, AT&T had to submit such plans for the utilization of its minority and female work forces. The GSA was responsible for approving these plans, and AT&T proceeded to deal with the GSA directly, apart from the FCC hearings.

The EEOC was aware of the current development of an af-

---

[10] *Ibid.*

firmative action plan by AT&T and had been assured that the GSA would not approve any plan without contacting the EEOC for its approval. It was a near breakdown in this agreement that spurred the government agencies to join forces and achieve a rapid settlement. In September 1972, the EEOC learned that the GSA had approved AT&T's affirmative action plan without consulting it.

The EEOC challenged the approved plan and lodged a complaint with the Department of Labor's Office of the Solicitor. The Department of Labor ruled that the GSA had not acted in the best interest of all parties and decided to enter the case itself. Within a short time, private negotiations were resumed, and the Departments of Labor and Justice joined the EEOC and AT&T as additional parties in the weekly negotiations.

The formal hearings recessed for Christmas and were scheduled to resume January 15, 1973, but were further postponed when word was given that the private negotiations had nearly come to an end. Then, on January 18, 1973, the settlement was announced, and the agreement was carried before Judge Leon A. Higginbotham in the U.S. District Court for the Eastern District of Pennsylvania.[11]

The final agreement was one developed in the informal negotiating sessions by all parties involved. The consent decree, as it came to be known, was formalized and agreed to slightly over two years after the EEOC petition to the FCC.

Benefits of the Decree to AT&T

Although the primary purpose of the consent decree from the government's point of view was to move AT&T's labor force toward "parity" employment (as we analyze in later chapters), AT&T derived several benefits by signing the consent decree. First, of course, the decree removed any threat of a cancellation of the rate increases granted by the FCC and opened the way for an early rate increase for the company.[12] Second, it eliminated for five years the potential for successful intervention on civil rights grounds before the FCC, or before any state regulatory commission, by a federal or state agency, or civil rights or other group, which might be designed to oppose or to thwart a proposed rate increase requested by AT&T

---

[11] *Equal Employment Opportunity Commission v. American Telephone & Telegraph Co.,* 365 F.Supp. 1105 (E.D. Pa. 1973), *aff'd in part, dismissed in part,* 506 F.2d 735 (3d Cir. 1974). See note 14 for the final disposition of the case.

[12] Although the effective date for the rate increase was moved forward to March 4, 1975, AT&T did receive an increase of 8.74 percent. Moreover, the FCC stated that it would hold hearings on an additional increase at a later date. See "FCC to Approve Phone-Rate Rise," *New York Times,* February 28, 1975, p. 1.

or one of its subsidiaries. As long as AT&T met its obligations under the consent decree, it was in effect protected against charges that it should not be granted otherwise deserved rate increases because it was violating public policy in regard to civil rights employment.

Third, this "legal umbrella" extended to other EEO-type charges as well. Individual charges of alleged discrimination were capable of being disproved by a showing that action comported to the decree's requirement. Finally, AT&T was able to "override" seniority, to favor minorities and women, and to otherwise engage in what might have been found to be "reverse discrimination," because it was operating pursuant to a court-sanctioned decree rather than merely following a company-instituted affirmative action plan. Moreover, AT&T's credibility with its employees to accomplish its goals was greatly enhanced by the fact that "it had no choice" and was only adhering to "the law of the land."

Supplemental Agreement

In May 1975, a supplemental agreement between the EEOC and AT&T was signed in the U.S. District Court in Philadelphia. This modification of the decree occurred because performance review of individual operating companies revealed that many intermediate targets had not been met. The agreement specified, by company, the race-sex deficiencies for each job class.

The agreement allowed for the prorating to other establishments within the same operating company of an establishment's deficiencies that remained as of December 31, 1976. To further insure that targets would be made, the agreement required the use of the affirmative action "override" in cases in which seniority agreements prevented the promotion of protected group workers. The agreement thus established the principle of "at least basically qualified" as the standard for the promotion of protected group workers and transformed the concept of intermediate targets into a *de facto* quota system which took precedence over existing collective bargaining procedures.

FEATURES OF THE DECREE

As a result of the decree, the Bell System labor force was partitioned into fifteen separate job classes ranging from management (job classes 1 through 3) to service workers (job class 15) (see Table I-1). The labor force was further segmented into ten race-sex groups, or five racial groups (Caucasian, Black, Hispanic, Asian Pacific, and Native American), for each sex.

TABLE I-1
AT&T Job Classifications

Job Class	Job Description
1	Upper-level management.
2	Middle-level management.
3	Entry-level management.
4	Administrative positions such as senior secretaries and supervisors. Also included here are advanced data processors.
5	Nonmanagerial sales workers. Included here are communications consultants, commercial representatives, and directory advertising salesmen.
6	Skilled outside craft workers such as PBX installers and repairmen.
7	Skilled inside craft workers such as switchmen.
8	Skilled general service employees including draftsmen, mechanics, and drivers.
9	Entry-level outside craft workers, primarily linemen.
10	Entry-level inside craft workers such as framemen.
11	Skilled clerical workers such as senior clerks, computer attendants, and service representatives.
12	Semiskilled clerical workers including stenographers and administrative clerks.
13	Entry-level clerical positions including typists and routing clerks.
14	Telephone operators.
15	Entry-level service workers such as cooks, elevator operators, and building maintenance.

Source: The Company.

Ultimate employment goals or ultimate objectives were then set for each of these ten groups in every job class. These goals were long-range ones as a result of which the race-sex profile of the AT&T labor force was eventually supposed to approximate that of the relevant labor pool. The objective is thus to achieve "statistical parity" in the labor force. (Although the term statistical parity conveys an aura of scientific precision, many of these goals were derived in bargaining.) In outside crafts, for example, the ultimate goal of 19 percent female representation was simply a compromise between the government's desire for a 38 percent utilization based upon the current labor force participation of women and the 3.8 percent figure for female utilization in outside crafts for the Bell System.

The process of transition from the 1973 labor force to an employee pool reflecting statistical parity was done through the attainment of intermediate targets. The establishment of these targets was accomplished by the GOALS 2 computer program that AT&T developed.

Simply stated, given operating company growth rates and statistics on employee turnover, GOALS 2 estimated the projected number of yearly openings by job class. These openings were further broken down into new hires and promotions. Once these opportunities were determined, current utilization of each race-sex group in the appropriate pool was compared with its ultimate goal. The end result was the establishment of yearly intermediate targets for each group. These targets were broken down into single targets for new hires and promotions. Operating companies were held strictly accountable for the attainment of these targets. Thus, in effect and results, targets became quotas. (For a more detailed description of this process, see Appendix I-A).

AT&T's performance in meeting its targets has been excellent. Although the company got off to a poor start by hitting only 51 percent of its goals in 1973, the situation was quickly reversed in successive years. In 1974, 90 percent of the targets were reached; in 1975, 97 percent. Since 1976, the company has done better than 99 percent each year.[13]

Affirmative Action Override

The achievement of intermediate targets conflicts with the time-honored principle of seniority. Consider a situation where GOALS 2 allocates three promotions to white females, ten to white males, and seven to the remaining race-sex groups. Let us suppose further that the twenty most-senior employees eligible for promotion are white males.

The operating company is caught on the horns of a dilemma here. If it adheres to its targets, it violates the seniority provisions of its collective bargaining agreements. If it follows seniority and promotes the twenty white males, it will not be in compliance with the terms of the decree.

The principal unions that represent AT&T employees challenged unsuccessfully the affirmative action override provision of the consent decree in the courts.[14] Seniority was thus made secondary to meeting the targets as explained below:

---

[13] Carol J. Loomis, "AT&T in the Throes of 'Equal Employment,' " *Fortune,* Vol. 99 (January 15, 1979), p. 50. We have been advised by company spokesmen that the *Fortune* analysis is correct.

[14] *Equal Employment Opportunity Commission v. American Telephone & Telegraph Co.,* 419 F.Supp. 1022 (E.D. Pa. 1976), *aff'd,* 556 F.2d 167 (3d Cir. 1977), *cert. denied,* 438 U.S. 915 (1978).

Broadly stated the override or affirmative action selection is one mechanism provided for in our January 18, 1973, Consent Decree to help meet our non-management EEO targets for minorities, and for white male and female non-traditional jobs. Where normal employment and selection routines, which include a major consideration for seniority, prevent us from fully meeting our targets for protected classes, we are obligated under the Decree to override senior qualified persons with junior *qualified* persons who are of the undertargeted race-sex group. Use of the override or affirmative action selection has been absolutely essential in helping our Companies meet their EEO targets.[15]

It should be noted, however, that the use of the override mechanism had decreased during the period of the consent decree. More and more targets have been attained without overriding the principle of seniority. Table I-2 presents the relevant data on the use of the override through 1976, the last period for which statistics are available.

Although Table I-2 shows an obvious decline in overrides since the 1973–74 period, the extent of the decline is questionable. One reason is that AT&T has provided data only for the blue-collar spectrum of its labor force—job classes 5 through 12. We have no statistics covering instances where management personnel have been passed over by less-senior or less-qualified employees. Another reason is that, after 1974, AT&T narrowed its definition of what constitutes an override. Previously, AT&T had counted as an override any promotion that was awarded to a less-senior or a less-qualified worker. Now, an override is said to have occurred only when the passed-over employee is covered by an existing labor contract.

Finally, AT&T is accused in a *Fortune* article of not counting all overrides, even those narrowly defined. *Fortune* estimated that the narrowly defined use of the override occurred approximately six thousand times per year since 1974. If these figures are correct, then the 1975–76 ratio of overrides to openings is 22 percent—not significantly different from the broadly defined level of 25.6 percent for the 1973–74 period.[16]

Upgrade and Transfer

The upgrade and transfer plan is designed to facilitate employee mobility throughout the Bell System at the nonmanagement level. The plan has been one of the most significant factors in the implementation of the consent decree.

---

[15] AT&T, "EEO Reference Binder," Section VIII, p. 1.
[16] Loomis, "AT&T in the Throes of 'Equal Employment,' " p. 54.

TABLE I-2
AT&T, Use of the Affirmative Action Override, 1973-76

	1973-74	1975	1976
Total openings in Job Classes 5-12	112,819	33,982	20,593
Total Use of the Override	28,856	4,529	2,094
Overrides as a Percentage of Total Openings	25.6	13.3	10.2

Source: The Company.

The focal point of the plan is the transfer bureau, a division of the personnel department designed to facilitate worker mobility within a given operating company. The bureau makes all selections for entry-level nonmanagement positions. For positions above entry level, individual departments have a voice in employee selection, but targets must be met. In addition, the transfer bureau publishes a list of projected job opportunities within the company for which all workers may compete. The pool of candidates considered for a given promotion has been expanded greatly because of the list.

To expedite the interdepartmental flow of employees, the concept of seniority has been broadened. Traditionally, seniority has been interpreted to mean departmental seniority. Under the expanded concept as specified in the decree, seniority is the length of service in any department within the Bell System. For example, a white female secretary may decide after a few years of service to request transfer to an outside craft position. If approved, her prior service as a secretary will count as seniority for promotion within outside crafts.

Two effects of this expanded concept of seniority are obvious. First, AT&T reduces its reliance on the use of the affirmative action override. Second, the potential exists for individuals to achieve promotion on total Bell or operating company experience but, at the same time, to lack needed experience in the particular job or area to which they are promoted.

Pay Adjustments

Much notoriety in the press has developed concerning compensation to be made to protected group workers as a result of past alleged AT&T discrimination. The final cost of these adjustments was estimated in 1974 at $45 million. This apparent liberality to a segment of the labor force would seem certain to increase adverse reactions among those not so favored. Whether by coincidence, the Bell System collective bargaining yielded more substantial results both on a real and comparative basis following the decree than it had before.

We may distinguish two major forms of compensation required by the consent decree. The first type consists of payments to females for differences between male-female wages for the same position.

> Previously promotion pay scales had been calculated so that employees obtaining promotions to a particular position from "male jobs" received a higher rate of pay than those transferred or promoted to the same position from the "female jobs." Thus, sex-typing of jobs at differential pay was perpetuated in the promotional procedures. The determinant of the wage of the newly promoted employee was the rate of pay in the previous position. This pay procedure resulted in females and males of the same length of service with the company, occupying the same position following transfer or promotion, but with the women compensated at a lower rate of pay.[17]

A second form of recompense involves the concept of delayed restitution. In operating companies with an underutilization of protected group workers, the presumption is made that this underutilization reflects discrimination in past promotion practices. Lump sum payments of $100 to $400 per employee were designed to alleviate the past effects of this alleged discrimination. Specifically, the decree stated that

> lump sum payments shall be made to each female and minority employee in each establishment where there exists in his or her respective job classification an underutilization of the group of which he or she is a member.[18]

To qualify for these lump sum payments, an employee must (1) have had four years of net credited service on July 1, 1971; (2) have been or will be promoted to a craft job subsequent to June 30, 1971, yet prior to July 1, 1974; and (3) remain in that craft job for at least six months. It was projected that these payments would be made to more than ten thousand workers.

Represcription

The consent decree provided for a reevaluation of targets and ultimate goals after three years of experience in pursuing af-

---

[17] Phyllis A. Wallace, "The Consent Decrees," in *Equal Employment Opportunity*, pp. 272–73.
[18] *Ibid.*, p. 273.

firmative action. The following points were formalized in a Memorandum of Agreement. The agreement was to be implemented by all operating companies in 1977.

1. Targets for protected groups were reduced for senior-level management (job classes 1 and 2).
2. Intermediate targets for minority group members who constituted less than 2 percent of the establishment work force were eliminated.
3. Targets for males in clerical positions (job classes 11 through 13) were also reduced.
4. The use of the affirmative action override was eliminated when a given race-sex group had attained 90 percent or more of its ultimate goal by the end of the previous year; however, the override would again be required should a race-sex group drop below 85 percent of its ultimate goal.
5. Job class 8, general services, was eliminated.

AFFIRMATIVE ACTION WITHOUT THE CONSENT DECREE

On January 18, 1979, the day after the termination of the consent decree, AT&T initiated its Model Affirmative Action Program. Relying on the lessons it had learned during the previous six years, AT&T's new approach to the accelerated advancement of protected group members combined the best features of the provisions of the consent decree with a commitment to good-faith efforts in the pursuit of equal employment opportunity.

Conspicuous by its absence in the new AT&T program is the requirement of an affirmative action override. The use of the override had been challenged unsuccessfully by the principal labor unions representing AT&T's employees. The denial of the primacy of seniority in cases where targets must be met had been a continual source of problems for the Bell System operating companies. It was therefore only logical to expect that the termination of the decree would be accompanied by the demise of the override.

Other key features of the decree, however, remain in the new program. Primary among these is the commitment to statistical parity.

> The equal employment objective for the Bell System and for each Operating Company is to achieve, within a reasonable period of time, an employee profile, with respect to race and sex in each major job classification, which is an approximate reflection of proper utilization.[19]

---

[19] AT&T, "A Model Affirmative Action Program for the Bell System," January 18, 1979, p. XI-1.

Utilization analyses will be prepared comparing the race-sex composition of an individual operating company's labor force with that of the underlying employment pool. From this, "numerical objectives" for protected group workers will be obtained.

The American Telephone and Telegraph Company recognizes that all numerical objectives explained in this section and detailed in the exhibits are neither rigid nor inflexible quotas, but objectives to be pursued by mobilization of available company resources for a "good faith effort."

At the termination of the 1973 EEO Consent Decree and Supplemental Order thereto, the express judicial requirement for preferential placement of members of certain race/sex groups ceased. Numerical objectives have been revised based on the anticipated impact of the absence of this requirement. Numerical objectives are projected and reviewed on an annual basis. The numerical objectives will be modified to assure that they provide maximum practical results toward our objective of achieving, within a reasonable period of time, an employee profile, with respect to sex and race in each major job classification, which is an approximate reflection of proper utilization. Further, modifications may also be made as they become necessary in light of the Company's experience in meeting numerical objectives in the absence of authority to exercise preferential placement.

The company will apply reasonable good faith efforts to meet any annual numerical objectives established as described herein.[20]

The numerical objectives are thus directly analogous to the intermediate targets established by the GOALS 2 program. Two main differences, however, exist between the present approach and that adopted during the decree:

1. The stress is on voluntarism and good-faith efforts in the attainment of numerical objectives. Internal EEO performance reviews will be employed to insure that adequate progress is being achieved.[21] Although external reporting to government agencies (principally annual EEO-1 and FCC-395 reports) will continue, the emphasis is placed on AT&T policing itself in a good-faith effort at affirmative action.[22]
2. There is a greater reliance on internal sources as the relevant labor pool.[23] As we note in chapter IV, attempts by AT&T to attain mandated targets by external hiring have been a major source of worker dissatisfaction.

In addition to numerical objectives, AT&T will continue to employ a transfer policy. This approach has proved extremely suc-

[20] *Ibid.*, p. V-1.
[21] *Ibid.*, p. VII-4.
[22] *Ibid.*, p. VII-2.
[23] *Ibid.*, p. XI-3.

cessful for the operating companies by insuring that larger pools of qualified applicants will be considered for a given advancement opportunity. On average, these larger applicant pools have led to an improvement in the caliber of those promoted within the Bell System.

A transfer plan operation will be used to facilitate meeting non-management staffing requirements. The purpose of the Plan is to provide a standardized and systematic selection process which applies the best qualified principle for filling all non-management jobs. Included with the process are (1) the means for employees to be considered for other jobs they may desire by specifying how their requests for such consideration are to be handled, (2) the means for management to identify and assess the qualifications of the current work force and (3) the means to assist the company in meeting its objective to provide equal employment opportunity without unlawful discrimination.[24]

As a final component in its affirmative action strategy, AT&T will continue to stress active community involvement with organizations such as the NAACP, the National Urban League, and the National Organization for Women.[25] The use of minority recruiters and speakers bureaus to attract protected group workers to the Bell System is also stressed.[26]

In summary, then, AT&T, in its new affirmative action program, has attempted to combine the best features of the consent decree with a stress on voluntarism. It remains to be seen, however, what will happen if the emphasis on good-faith efforts fails to sustain the progress achieved under the decree.

24 *Ibid.*, p. VI-6.
25 *Ibid.*, p. VI-2.
26 *Ibid.*, p. VIII-2.

Appendix I–A

GOALS 2

Figure I-A-1 contains a flow chart covering the GOALS 2 allocation process. Although the actual program is divided into three separate parts, only the first two are of interest to us.

The first stage of the program determines the number of employment opportunities projected for an individual operating company during a given year. These opportunities are then allocated between hires and promotions. The promotion process has been the greater source of friction at AT&T.

Promotions

For purposes of illustration, we examine how the number of black males promoted to second-level management is determined. To do this, three measures are needed:
1. the percentage of black males in the job class where the given advancement opportunity lies,
2. the percentage of black males in the qualified regional labor force, and
3. the ultimate utilization goal for black males in the job class where the opening lies.

A ratio of (1) is taken to the smaller of (2) and (3), and a percentage is computed. A low value for this percentage indicates an underutilization of black males relative to their representation in the qualified labor force. The percentage thus obtained yields a multiplier which will be used in allocating targets to black males.

For example, suppose that there will be ten openings in second-level management in a given year. At the present time, ten black males are second-level managers out of a total of one hundred. Thus, 10 percent of second-level managers are black males. Suppose further that 15 percent of the qualified labor force is black males. Then, the ratio of AT&T's utilization to black male representation in the qualified labor pool is 66 percent (10 percent divided by 15 percent). The flow chart shows that GOALS 2 assigns this value to a multiplier of 1.5.

Because the ultimate goal is 15 percent, GOALS 2 will allocate to black males 23 percent of all openings (1.5 times 15 percent). Thus, two black males will be promoted to second-level management. Once all promotions have been completed, any remaining openings are filled by hiring new personnel in accordance with Part II, B, of the chart.

FIGURE I-A-1
GOALS 2

1. DETERMINE PROJECTED OPPORTUNITIES

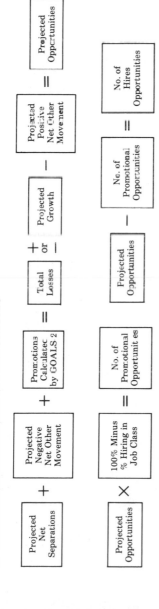

2. DETERMINE ALLOCATIONS OF PROJECTED OPPORTUNITIES

A. PROMOTIONS

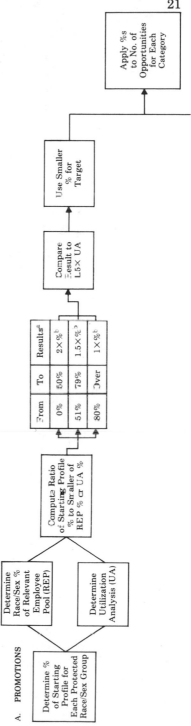

FIGURE I-A-1 (continued)

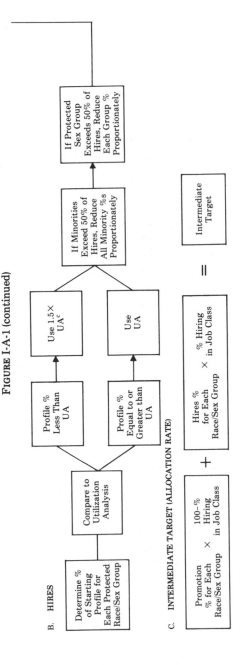

B. HIRES

C. INTERMEDIATE TARGET (ALLOCATION RATE)

$$\text{Promotion \% for Each Race/Sex Group} \times \text{100-\% Hiring in Job Class} + \text{Hires \% for Each Race/Sex Group} \times \text{\% Hiring in Job Class} = \text{Intermediate Target}$$

3. DETERMINE END OF YEAR TARGET PROFILE

$$\text{Starting Profile} - \text{Total Losses} + \text{Positive Net Other Movement and Profiles of Promoted and Hired Groups} = \text{Year End Target Profile}$$

Source: The Company.

[a] Job classes 1 and 2—Maximum multiple of 1.5 for all protected groups. Job classes 11, 12, and 13—Maximum multiplier of 1 for all male groups.

[b] Percent being the smaller of the REP or the UA.

[c] For males in job classes 11, 12, 13, and 14, a maximum multiplier of 1 will always be used.

CHAPTER II

AT&T in the Modern Telecommunications Industry

To appreciate properly the magnitude of the problem faced by AT&T in the implementation of the consent decree, several facts about the modern telecommunications industry must be understood. Specifically, the telecommunications industry during the 1970s was simultaneously a rapidly expanding and a rapidly declining sector of the economy. Imbedded in the apparent paradox of the last sentence are the twin forces that have shaped the industry during the last ten years: the acceleration of technological progress and the development of new sources of competition.

Technological advances, especially in the field of data processing, have opened up new markets, leading to rapid growth for AT&T. Coupled with this, however, have been several FCC decisions that have paved the way for the entry of potential competitors with the Bell System.

Rapid growth through technical progress and the necessity of obtaining increased efficiency in order to stave off the forces of competition have contributed to the paradox of decline in the midst of growth. Decline, in this case, is a decrease in employment opportunities and a change in the composition of total employment.

In short, what we observe at AT&T is the coexistence of tremendous growth in output markets and a decline in the need for labor services in the input markets. AT&T's problems with the implementation of the consent decree are thus compounded. Not only must it pursue affirmative action, but it must do so in the context of a declining labor force.

In this chapter, we begin by examining some significant indicators of growth experienced by AT&T during 1973–79, the period of the consent decree. We also note the changing employment mix and discuss the reasons for this. We conclude with a projection of future trends and the effects these will have on the composition of the labor force in the Bell System.

AT&T PERFORMANCE ANALYSIS, 1973-79

By any objective standard, the period 1973–79 was one of high profitability and growth for the Bell System. Tables II-1 and II-2 present some significant statistics in this regard. All figures listed in the tables are in $1,000 units and are taken from reports filed with the Securities and Exchange Commission (Form 10-K) covering AT&T and its consolidated subsidiaries. Note that physical plant and total assets are listed at historical cost.

Table II-1 indicates significant growth in output. Operating revenues rose by over 74 percent for the period 1973–78. This yields a yearly growth rate of 11.7 percent, which far outstrips inflation. Physical plant and total assets also increased at yearly rates that exceeded 9 percent.

The above measures, however, tell little about the key variable, profitability. Physical growth is meaningless if it leads to a decline in profits. As Table II-2 demonstrates, AT&T performance with respect to the key variable has also been impressive.

We thus see that profitability has kept pace with physical growth. Key market indicators such as earnings per share and return to equity (net income divided by owner's equity) showed significant increases during the period covered. Most important, net income rose by 75.9 percent over this time. Its annual rate of growth, 12 percent, also exceeded the average inflation rate for this period. These gains are thus indicative of real increases as opposed to mere paper profits brought about by inflation.

Given this growth in profitability and output, we must next examine AT&T's input markets during this period. We have already considered part of this question above when we noted the 54.3 percent increase in physical plant. Given this increase in capital inputs, we must next ask what effect this has had on the Bell System's demand for labor.

CHANGES IN THE AT&T LABOR FORCE, 1973-79

While output, profitability, and physical plant all increased during the period 1973–79, the opposite effect was observed in the AT&T labor force. We have aggregated all AT&T employees into eight occupational groups. Table II-3 lists the job classes found in each group. In this section, we consider only changes in the size of the labor force. The alteration in the composition of the employment pool is discussed later in this chapter. Table II-4 presents a breakdown of the AT&T labor force on December 31, 1973, and on January 17, 1979, the termination date of the decree.

TABLE II-1
AT&T, Systems Growth Measures

	1973	1978	Percent Change
Operating Revenues	23,527,320	40,993,356	74.2
Physical Plant	58,568,065	90,351,525	54.3
Total Assets	67,051,114	103,326,945	54.1

Source: The Company.

TABLE II-2
AT&T, Systems Profitability Measures

	1973	1979	Percent Change
Net Income	2,997,716	5,272,606	75.9
Owner's Equity	31,223,295	40,618,208	30.1
Earnings per Share	5.0	7.7	54.8
Percent Return to Equity	9.6	13.0	

Source: The Company.
Note: Owner's equity and net income are both expressed in $1,000 units.

TABLE II-3
AT&T, Labor Force, Occupational Group and Job Classes

Occupational Group	Job Classes
Officials and Managers	1, 2, 3
Administrative	4
Sales Workers	5
Clerical	11, 12, 13
Operators	14
Outside Crafts	6, 9
Inside Crafts	7, 10
Service Workers	8, 15

Source: The Company.

While output and profitability measures were rising, AT&T was able to substitute capital for labor and thereby reduce its labor force growth to 0.2 percent, an increase of only 1,270 jobs. White-collar employment, other than operator, increased by 56,387, but this was counterbalanced by a decrease of 55,117 positions among other occupational groups.

TABLE II-4
AT&T, Labor Force, December 31, 1973–January 15, 1979

Occupational Group	1973	1979	Percent Change
Officials and Managers	164,438	191,436	16.4
Administrative	30,135	33,913	12.5
Sales Workers	7,038	8,999	27.9
Clerical	207,461	231,111	11.4
Operators	143,918	102,654	-28.7
Total White Collar	552,990	568,113	2.8
Outside Crafts	136,391	135,072	-1.0
Inside Crafts	97,198	97,569	0.4
Service Workers	24,003	11,098	-53.8
Total Blue Collar	257,592	243,739	-5.4
Total Employment	810,582	811,852	0.2

Source: The Company.

The bulk of this reduction occurred among operators where a net loss of 41,264 positions was experienced. This decrease is consistent with a trend first observed in 1957[1] and is the result of technological progress as switching devices replace workers and of the institution of charges for information, which greatly reduces such calls and the consequent need for operators.

Unionization

It should be noted that 460,000 of the telephone workers are represented by the Communications Workers of America (CWA). Another 70,000 workers are represented by the International Brotherhood of Electrical Workers (IBEW). Although independent unions exist, the CWA and the IBEW are clearly the dominant labor unions within the Bell System.[2]

The leadership of the unions is heavily dominated by white males. There is some white female representation in the union hierarchy, particularly in the CWA, but blacks and other minorities are conspicuous by their absence. The implications of this for labor relations in an affirmative action context are discussed below.

The unions bargain with AT&T for long-distance workers and with the operating companies for individual employees. Since 1974,

[1] L. Earl Lewis and Joseph C. Bush, "Employment and Wage Trends in Bell System Companies," *Monthly Labor Review,* Vol. 90, No. 3 (March 1967), p. 39.

[2] "Unions Scramble for Power in Communications," *Business Week,* May 1, 1978, p. 83.

wage and key issue bargaining has taken place at the national level. Counterbalancing these increases in the power of organized labor are the standard problems posed for unionization as a result of changes in the composition of the labor force. Table II-4 shows that telephone operators and blue-collar workers, the traditional job categories for union organization, were reduced by 55,117 positions at AT&T between 1973 and 1979.

Wage Structure

In the 1970s, significant advances in wages paid within the telephone industry have occurred. Hourly rates of pay increases to telephone workers (and to line construction employees—a skilled component of the telephone industry labor force) far outpaced the gains experienced by workers in other public utilities (see Table II-5). Whereas in 1970, wages of telephone workers were substantially below those of electric and gas company employees, by 1978, telephone wages exceeded those of gas companies and were virtually even with those of electric utilities.

Several factors could be responsible for these changes. An obvious one is that AT&T remained quite prosperous throughout this period, whereas many electric and gas utilities suffered from greatly enhanced fuel prices, flat demand, and the insensitivity of state regulatory commissions to their plight. Whether the payments to women and minorities induced unions in the Bell System to stiffen demands and encouraged the companies to liberalize offers in order to reduce disquiet during the period of the consent decree could not definitely be discerned.

We now examine in greater detail the forces of technological progress within the telecommunications industry. For it is only by understanding these forces that we can appreciate why the change in the AT&T labor force has occurred. More important, the implications of technical progress will place severe constraints on the ability of AT&T to implement affirmative action plans in the future.

THE EFFECT OF TECHNICAL PROGRESS
ON THE LABOR FORCE

Technical progress accomplishes two things, both of which can be seen by a careful examination of Table II-4 above. First, technical progress allows fewer workers to provide greater output. Hence, we see during our period a 74 percent increase in operating revenues occurring concurrently with a 0.2 percent increase in the size of the AT&T labor force.

TABLE II-5
Hourly Wages in Selected Public Utilities, 1970–78

Public Utility Employees	1970	1978	Percent Yearly Growth Rate
All Telephone	$3.43	$7.67	10.6
Line Construction	4.21	9.61	10.9
Electric Company	4.30	7.84	7.8
Gas Company	3.60	7.39	9.4

Source: U.S., Department of Labor, Bureau of Labor Statistics, *Employment and Earnings*, Vol. 18, No. 12 (1971), Table C-2, p. 90; Vol. 25, No. 12 (1978), Table C-2, p. 96.

In addition, technical progress changes the composition of the labor force. The modern telephone worker will have to be more sophisticated in order to operate the more technically sophisticated equipment. Greater emphasis will be placed on managerial and administrative skills. As Table II-4 points out, both these groups increased in employment during our period of examination.

Let us analyze both of these effects in greater detail. We begin by discussing the ability of technical advances to reduce the labor force. From the myriad of possible technical improvements, we shall focus on four: underground cabling, phone jacks, the Traffic Service Position System, and electrical switching systems. This substitution of capital for labor has occurred mainly at the blue-collar and operator levels.

In addition, although it is not directly concerned with technical progress, we also note in passing how decisions of state regulatory boards, specifically, permission to charge for directory assistance, can reduce the size of the labor force.

Underground Cabling

The use of underground cabling has resulted in lower maintenance and replacement requirements and has thereby reduced the demand for outside craft workers. The problem for outside craft workers will be compounded with the increasing use of microwave relays and satellite systems for communications.[3]

These systems are also characterized by lower maintenance requirements and have the ability to handle larger volumes of calls than present wires and coaxial cables. Thus, as the new technology replaces that presently in use, the need for installation and repair

---

[3] "Ma Bell Fights off Invasion of Her Domain," *U.S. News & World Report*, August 14, 1978, p. 55.

workers will decline, and those who do find employment must display a greater technical capacity.

Phone Jacks

A similar reduction in the demand for outside craft workers will occur as a result of the expanded use of phone jacks, especially in the consumer market.

> Today the Bell companies are installing about 150,000 jacks in home and business offices every working day, giving customers greater flexibility in the use of their telephone service. Customers whose homes are thus equipped can install the phone themselves, thereby saving part of the service connection charge.[4]

Needless to say, this savings on connection charges comes at the expense of jobs in outside crafts.

It should be noted that the recent decision of the FCC permitting telephone users to buy their own telephones will necessarily increase the use of phone jacks in the consumer market. It has been estimated that this decision will open up a market with a yearly sales potential of $1 billion, a figure which will exceed 10 percent of all yearly equipment sales.[5] This will further reduce the need for outside craft workers.

Traffic Service Position System

The Traffic Service Position System (TSPS) has contributed substantially to the reduction in the need for telephone operators. Bell of Pennsylvania is a case in point:

> The year 1965 also marked the cutover in Pennsylvania of the first installation of Traffic Service Positions to facilitate customer dialing of person-to-person, collect and credit card calls. Five years later an improved version, the Traffic Service Position System (TSPS), which utilizes Electronic Switching technology, went into service to serve the remainder of Philadelphia. TSPS installations have rapidly replaced the old cord boards throughout the Company. A total of 800 positions are now in operation, and, within the next 12 months, about 70 per cent of operator-handled calls will be routed by TSPS. By the end of the 1979, that figure will increase to almost 85 percent.[6]

Electronic Switching Systems

Electronic switching systems (ESS) provide operational savings resulting from reduced maintenance and manpower requirements

[4] *American Telephone and Telegraph Company 1977 Annual Report*, pp. 12–14.
[5] "The New New Telephone Industry," *Business Week*, February 13, 1978, p. 68.
[6] *Bell of Pennsylvania Annual Report 1977*.

and greatly reduce the need for operators. Again, we consider the case of Bell of Pennsylvania:

> In addition to the dial central offices equipped with ESS, two new 4E toll switching stations were placed in service in 1977. Located in Wayne and Pittsburgh, they are the very latest in communications technology. The 4E can handle 550,000 phone calls an hour, five times the capacity of the unit it replaced. Moreover, it takes only half the building space, half the manpower, and far less energy. As others come on line, we can reduce the overall number of toll switchers in Pennsylvania dramatically.[7]

Directory Assistance Charging

It should be noted that there are forces in addition to technology that are contributing to the reduced need for telephone workers. Particularly important are decisions of state regulatory boards to permit a charge for directory assistance. Southwestern Bell illustrates the point:

> In Missouri, for instance, when directory assistance charging became effective, call volumes fell more than 50 percent almost immediately. As a result, we need fewer directory assistance operators, and our expenses in Missouri will be $5.1 million lower than they would have been without directory assistance charging.[8]

Positive Labor Force Impacts

Although closing many avenues of employment, the new telecommunications technology has also opened up many new opportunities within AT&T. In particular, the opportunities for technically trained managers have significantly increased.

Table II-6 shows a significant shift toward management positions over the five-year period. Opportunities for administrative and clerical workers have also risen. In 1973, 49.6 percent of the labor force was either blue collar or operator; five years later, these same groups accounted for only 47.6 percent of the same labor force.

To summarize, then, technology has shifted the employment concentration away from operators and blue-collar workers and toward the management ranks. Concurrent with this has been a rise in clerical and administrative employment. (Sales workers have also risen in absolute and percentage terms). As will be seen below, however, this can best be explained by the changing competitive structure of the telecommunications industry.

---

[7] *Ibid.*
[8] *Southwestern Bell Annual Report 1976,* p. 11.

TABLE II-6
AT&T, Labor Force, Percent Distribution
December 1973–January 1979

Occupational Group	Percent of Total	
	1973	1979
Officials and Managers	20.3	23.6
Administrative	3.7	4.2
Sales Workers	0.9	1.1
Clerical	25.6	28.5
Operators	17.8	12.6
Total White Collar	68.3	70.0
Outside Crafts	16.8	16.6
Inside Crafts	12.0	12.0
Service Workers	2.9	1.4
Total Blue Collar	31.7	30.0

Source: The Company.

IMPLICATIONS FOR FUTURE LABOR DEMAND

What implications does our discussion have for the type of worker who will make a significant contribution to the Bell System in the future? During the last nine years, there has clearly been an increased need for managerial personnel. In order to administer a technologically sophisticated communications system, managers must display an increasingly analytical expertise. The future AT&T administrator must feel at home in a world of lightwave systems, long-life lasers, computers, microprocessors, and communications satellites.

The new technology has not exempted the blue-collar worker from changes. While eliminating many jobs, it has drastically increased the skill requirements for craft work. All operating companies report increased training expenditures to upgrade the skill levels of employees. For prospective new employees in crafts, technical expertise is a prerequisite for selection.

But what of the future? Will the demands of technology diminish over time? Clearly the answer is no. In fact, if anything, they will increase. Opportunities for operators and craft workers will continue to decline as the technological advances in communications continue to gain wider usage. Prospects for technically trained managerial personnel will continue to be good. In particular, the marriage of the communications industry with the expanding field of data processing offers many exciting prospects for future employment growth.

Thus in the next few years, the growth of new information systems based on communications networks could make the first two decades of the electronic data-processing industry look like a warm-up. Increasingly, executives in both the phone and computer industries tend to agree that it is a mix of their two businesses that will lead, finally, to practical electronic funds transfer systems for corporations, and the so-called office of the future.[9]

This emerging computer-communications market growth has been estimated at between 15 and 20 percent per year for the next ten to twenty years. AT&T is forecasting market revenues of about $380 billion for this segment by the early 1990s.[10]

The implications of these changes are clear. Employment prospects at AT&T for managers and technicians with computer backgrounds will grow as the Bell System moves into this expanding market. In all the field interviews conducted by the authors with senior personnel officers in various operating companies, the same refrain was heard: "We are suffering from a shortage of personnel with strong computer science backgrounds." This dearth was especially noticeable at the managerial level.

In a consideration of affirmative action, the key question becomes the extent and quality of the supply of protected group workers with the appropriate technical and computer backgrounds to fill these new openings. If there are too few qualified protected group members available for the jobs developed by the modern telecommunications industry, affirmative action will have a minimal impact on the long-run race-sex profile of the AT&T labor force.

COMPETITION IN COMMUNICATIONS

In recent years, rigorous competition has emerged in what has traditionally been a regulated industry. The development of competition poses obvious potential problems for the Bell System. We focus on two: the conflict between AT&T and the computer industries in the expanding data processing market and the emergence of the specialized common carrier. The problem is basically the same in both instances; namely, a highly regulated firm, AT&T, competing against firms that operate in a comparatively free environment.

---

9 "The New New Telephone Industry," p. 68.
10 *Ibid.*, p. 70.

Computers and Communication

A potential overlap exists between the market served by the computer industry and that served by AT&T.

> "Right now there is utter chaos in the marketplace," warns consultant W. Porter Stone. The fast-moving technology, he explains, is making it impossible for the FCC and the courts to draw a hard line between computers, which are unregulated, and communications, which is regulated. "But monopoly and competition can't operate in the same marketplace," he says.[11]

The main competition in this area is the computer giant, International Business Machines. Other firms include Litton Industries, International Telephone and Telegraph, and Southern Pacific. This threat has led AT&T to place increased emphasis on marketing its product. Table II-4 shows a substantial growth in the sales worker group. Opportunities will continue in this area as AT&T strives to meet further competition. An implication of the following quotation, however, is that marketing expertise must be buttressed by significant technical knowledge of the product to be marketed. Thus, even in the area of sales, a strong technological background is a prerequisite.

> Fearing IBM's strength, AT&T has bolstered its corporate marketing operations with several hundred recruits, *many from suppliers of data processing equipment.* And it has put more marketing troops in the field. Four years ago, the Bell System's 23 operating companies did not even include the title of vice-president or director of marketing or sales on their executive rosters. Now each has a marketing officer.[12]

This increased emphasis on marketing and "The System is the Solution" should enable AT&T to maintain a strong position in the developing communications-data processing market. The role of the specialized common carriers, our second example of competition, poses a stronger potential problem for AT&T.

The Interconnect Industry

The specialized common carrier brings the threat of competition to the long-distance phone market. In order to provide low-cost local calls, AT&T charges rates in excess of a normal return on the cost of a long-distance telephone call. This excess return is used as a subsidy to provide low-cost local service, an objective of the FCC.

Specialized common carriers offer a service to the high volume

---

[11] *Ibid.*, p. 71.
[12] *Ibid.*, p. 69 (emphasis supplied).

users of long-distance calls, which are typically businesses. These carriers can connect the firm to the lines of the Bell System (permitted under FCC rulings) for the placement of long-distance calls. Hence, the term "interconnect industry." Because the carrier does not have to subsidize local calls, it is able to charge a long-distance rate that competes favorably with that offered by the Bell System.

Typical of these interconnect firms is MCI Communications Corporation.

> Several other firms are also taking advantage of this newer and inherently cheaper method by providing long-distance service at rates up to 30 percent lower than those charged by AT&T.
> Leading the way is a firm called MCI Communications Corporation, which operates in 40 major cities. MCI sells private-line service to · companies that want direct phone lines between their head and branch offices. Companies conducting large amounts of nationwide business thus have a cheaper alternative to Bell's WATS service, which allows toll-free long-distance calling for a flat monthly rate.[13]

Legal questions regarding the approval of such carrier services and the rates to be charged have yet to be completely resolved. The FCC has promised further hearings on the matter. One point, however, is clear. The Bell System is extremely worried about this aspect of increasing competition. The tone of the following quotation taken from the annual report of Southwestern Bell is typical of that found in the reports of other operating companies discussing this issue.

> These new firms, usually called specialized common carriers, have chosen to serve high-profit private line routes and high-profit customers. Not having to serve the home telephone customer—and not wanting to—new carriers can zero in on the lucrative markets that make low rates possible. In simple words, this is cream-skimming.
> If the FCC continues these policies of market allocation that lead to cream-skimming, the result will be that the telephone industry . . . will be forced more and more to base prices on costs to avoid losing revenues to the new carriers. . . .
> Cost studies indicate that cost-based pricing would mean substantial price increases for an estimated 90 percent of the country's households.
> We don't believe this social result is in the public interest.[14]

SUMMARY

We have seen the effect of technology and competition on AT&T and have considered projections of future trends in these two key areas of the modern telecommunications industry.

---

13 "Ma Bell Fights off Invasion of Her Domain," p. 56.
14 *Southwestern Bell Annual Report 1976*, pp. 2–3.

Technological change will continue to reduce the blue-collar and operator labor forces. Electronic switching systems now serve only 24 percent of Bell customers.[15] As this percentage increases, blue-collar demand will fall. Those who do find jobs in this area will have to demonstrate increased technical capacity to service and to operate modern telecommunications equipment. Familiarity with data processing and computer maintenance will become an increasingly desired employment skill.

Managerial opportunities for technically trained professionals will continue to expand. Increasingly, a strong background in computer science will be required as AT&T tries to protect its position in what *Business Week* calls "the nation's fastest growing new market."[16] A technical aptitude will be a prerequisite for entry and advancement at AT&T in both managerial and blue-collar ranks.

Competition, on the other hand, will continue to place demands on marketing personnel to demonstrate that the system is, in fact, the solution. Effective marketing in a highly technical industry will also require a strong technological background. Thus, even in marketing, prospective employees will have to demonstrate a strong technical aptitude.

Emerging competition will also increase the pace of technical change as AT&T strives to stay ahead of its rivals. Competition poses the threat of premature obsolescence for a major part of current telephone equipment as efficiency considerations become paramount.[17] Thus, competition will hasten the effects of the substitution of capital for labor.

The above analysis has concentrated on the demand side of the labor market. The key question of supply—particularly the supply of technically trained protected group members—remains to be considered. If there is not a sufficient pool of technically qualified minorities and white females, the efforts of AT&T (and other firms) to implement affirmative action in an increasingly competitive and efficiency-oriented industrial environment will be thwarted.

---

[15] *American Telephone and Telegraph Company 1977 Annual Report*, p. 9.
[16] "The New New Telephone Industry," p. 68.
[17] *Ibid.*

CHAPTER III

The Overall Impact

In this chapter, we examine the changes that have occurred in the race-sex composition of the AT&T labor force during the period of the consent decree and the impact of those changes on the company. Because the data reveal different, but important, patterns depending on the level of aggregation, the results presented in this chapter are at the national level. Chapter IV examines the same data by geographical region.

We divide the AT&T labor force into four racial groups by sex. We thus have a total of eight groups for analysis: black males, black females, white females, white males, Hispanic males, Hispanic females, other males, and other females. Hispanics and other minorities are, however, combined in several tables under the "other minority" category.

Although data are initially presented for the eight occupational groups introduced in the previous chapter, we confine the major part of our analysis to the following job classifications: officials and managers, sales workers, clerical, outside crafts, and inside crafts. This is done on the projection that these groups represent the keystone of the future AT&T labor force. First, however, we present the overall participation and distribution data for 1973 and 1979 in order to show changes that have occurred as a result of the consent decree.

THE GENERAL PICTURE

Table III-1 compares the number and percentage of employees for 1973 and 1979 in the Bell System by race and by eight occupational groups. These data show substantial percentage gains by blacks and other minorities (including Hispanic) in all white-collar occupations except operator. In that category, other minorities increased their share of jobs while the percentage of blacks declined. Because blacks were only concentrated as operators, the results represent an upgrading and thus a real gain, not a loss.

TABLE III-1

AT&T, Employment by Race and Occupational Group
1973 and 1979

Occupational Group	Total	1973 Black	Percent Black	Other Minorities	Percent Other Minorities
Officials and Managers	164,438	4,557	2.8	2,286	1.4
Administrative	30,135	2,596	8.6	597	2.0
Sales Workers	7,038	541	7.7	214	3.0
Clerical	207,461	31,512	15.2	11,336	5.5
Operators	143,918	28,430	19.8	6,060	4.2
Total White Collar	552,990	67,636	12.2	20,493	3.7
Outside Crafts	136,391	7,905	5.8	4,609	3.4
Inside Crafts	97,198	5,981	6.2	3,432	3.5
Service Workers	24,003	6,245	26.0	1,675	7.0
Total Blue Collar	257,592	20,131	7.8	9,716	3.8
Total	810,582	87,767	10.8	30,209	3.7

	Total	Black	Percent Black	Other Minorities	Percent Other Minorities
			1979		
Officials and Managers	191,436	10,821	5.7	5,959	3.1
Administrative	33,913	4,619	13.6	1,369	4.0
Sales Workers	8,999	1,215	13.5	441	4.9
Clerical	231,111	42,433	18.4	16,965	7.3
Operators	102,654	19,946	19.4	6,188	6.0
Total White Collar	568,113	79,034	13.9	30,922	5.4
Outside Crafts	135,072	8,419	6.2	6,240	4.6
Inside Crafts	97,569	7,918	8.1	4,454	4.6
Service Workers	11,098	3,062	27.6	896	8.1
Total Blue Collar	243,739	19,399	8.0	11,590	4.8
Total	811,852	98,433	12.1	42,512	5.2

Source: The Company.

In the blue-collar area, the situation is different. Blacks made few gains and failed to enhance their position in the key area of outside crafts. They did somewhat better in inside crafts, which accounted for virtually all their improvement in the blue-collar occupations. Other minorities, however, made gains in all three blue-collar occupational groups. It should be noted that these minority gains occurred despite a growth of only 1,270, or 0.2 percent, in total employment during the five-year period of the consent decree.

Male Minorities

Table III-2 provides the same data for males. Again, blacks and other minorities made real gains in their share of the top three salaried job groups. In clerical work, black males remained about even, as did other minority males; in the operator position, black males saw their shares reduced somewhat, but other minorities made a sizable gain.

In the blue-collar areas, black males held their own in outside crafts and made gains in inside crafts and in the less desirable service workers category. Overall, the share of work of blacks in blue-collar jobs declined, a sharp contrast to the white-collar situation. Other minorities gained in all blue-collar occupations. These changes occurred while male employment was relatively steady and rose by only 4,734 persons, or one percent.

Female Minorities

Table III-3 provides the relevant employment data for females. It must be considered in the light of a 3,464, or 0.3 percent, decline in female employment between 1973 and 1979.

Black females made sharp percentage gains in the top three salaried positions, increased their share of clerical jobs, and almost maintained their share of operator jobs. Other minorities followed a somewhat similar pattern, except for gains in the operator classification. Overall, the position both of black females and other minority females were enhanced in the salaried groups.

In the blue-collar classifications, black female participation in outside crafts doubled; it increased in inside crafts and stayed almost equal among service workers. Because of the relative size of the service worker population, however, the combined blue-collar segment shows a slight decline in black female participation. Other minorities showed gains in all categories.

TABLE III-2

AT&T, Male Employment by Race and Occupational Group
1973 and 1979

| Occupational Group | Male | Percent Male | 1973 | | | | |
			Black	Percent Black	Other Minorities	Percent Other Minorities
Officials and Managers	124,092	75.5	2,167	1.8	1,384	1.1
Administrative	5,770	19.0	350	6.1	150	2.6
Sales Workers	4,394	62.4	250	5.7	112	2.6
Clerical	12,254	5.9	1,689	13.8	1,341	10.9
Operators	6,445	4.5	900	14.0	592	9.2
Total White Collar	152,875	27.6	5,356	3.5	3,579	2.3
Outside Crafts	135,419	99.3	7,848	5.8	4,573	3.4
Inside Crafts	86,757	89.3	4,841	5.0	3,088	3.2
Service Workers	18,460	76.9	4,682	25.4	1,460	7.9
Total Blue Collar	240,656	93.4	17,371	7.2	9,121	3.8
Total	393,511	48.5	22,727	5.8	12,700	3.2

Table III-2 (continued)

Occupational Group	Male	Percent Male	Black	Percent Black	Other Minorities	Percent Other Minorities
				1979		
Officials and Managers	135,726	70.1	5,194	3.8	3,589	2.6
Administrative	8,473	25.0	711	8.4	372	4.4
Sales Workers	4,951	55.0	510	10.3	242	4.9
Clerical	25,626	11.1	3,506	13.7	2,734	10.7
Operators	8,068	7.9	1,147	14.2	872	10.8
Total White Collar	182,844	32.2	11,068	6.1	7,809	4.3
Outside Crafts	128,759	95.3	7,677	6.0	5,807	4.5
Inside Crafts	80,063	82.1	5,499	6.9	3,382	4.2
Service Workers	6,579	59.3	1,863	28.3	619	9.4
Total Blue Collar	215,401	88.4	15,039	7.0	9,808	4.6
Total	398,245	49.1	26,107	6.6	17,617	4.4

Source: The Company.

TABLE III-3

AT&T, Female Employment by Race and Occupational Group
1973 and 1979

Occupational Group	1973					
	Female	Percent Female	Black	Percent Black	Other Minorities	Percent Other Minorities
Officials and Managers	40,346	24.5	2,390	5.9	902	2.2
Administrative	24,425	81.1	2,246	9.2	447	1.8
Sales Workers	2,644	57.6	251	9.5	102	3.9
Clerical	195,207	94.1	29,823	15.3	9,995	5.1
Operators	137,493	95.5	27,530	20.0	5,468	4.0
Total White Collar	400,115	72.4	62,240	15.6	16,914	4.2
Outside Crafts	972	0.7	57	5.9	36	3.7
Inside Crafts	10,441	10.7	1,140	10.9	344	3.3
Service Workers	5,543	23.1	1,563	28.2	215	3.9
Total Blue Collar	16,956	6.6	2,760	16.3	595	3.5
Total	417,071	51.5	65,000	15.6	17,509	4.2

TABLE III-3 (continued)

Occupational Group	1979					
	Female	Percent Female	Black	Percent Black	Other Minorities	Percent Other Minorities
Officials and Managers	55,710	29.1	5,627	10.1	2,370	4.3
Administrative	25,440	75.0	3,908	15.4	997	3.9
Sales Workers	4,048	45.0	705	17.4	199	4.9
Clerical	205,485	88.9	38,927	18.9	14,231	6.9
Operators	94,586	92.1	18,799	19.9	5,316	5.6
Total White Collar	385,269	67.8	67,966	17.6	23,113	6.0
Outside Crafts	6,313	4.7	742	11.8	433	6.9
Inside Crafts	17,506	17.9	2,419	13.8	1,072	6.1
Service Workers	4,519	40.7	1,199	26.5	277	6.1
Total Blue Collar	28,338	11.6	4,360	15.4	1,782	6.3
Total	413,607	50.9	72,326	17.5	24,895	6.0

Source: The Company.

Females as a Class

As emphasized in chapter I, the consent decree was at least as much directed toward females as toward minorities. Table III-4 looks at females as a class without regard to race. Surprisingly, until one looks deeper, the percentage for female salaried workers declined from 72.4 percent in 1973 to 67.8 percent in 1979. This was true despite increases in the female share of officials and managers and sales worker positions. The female percentage declined for the administrative, clerical, and operator groups, which comprise the bulk of salaried workers.

The decline in female workers is in accord with the consent decree's objective of reducing the female concentrations in traditional female jobs. Clerical and operator positions, which were once virtually all female, now have a male minority. Administrative jobs, which include many traditional female jobs—e.g., service supervisors, executive secretaries, senior clerks—now have also had males assigned to them for the first time. Increased participation was not the only goal of the consent decree advocates; integration even at the expense of protected groups was equally important in their minds, particularly in regard to females. Table III-4 provides evidence of the success of this philosophy.

The blue-collar data in Table III-4 demonstrates further the integration results of the consent decree. Outside crafts, once the bulwark of the male, was 4.7 percent female by 1979. (We discuss the service cost of this below.) The inside craft and service worker groups saw significant percentage gains for females, resulting in a one-third increase in the overall share of blue-collar jobs for females.

Thus, females gained in nontraditional females jobs and lost in traditional ones. The new result, however, when combined with the drop in employment, which was heavily concentrated in the traditional female operator classification, resulted in a decline in overall female workers from 51.5 to 50.9 percent. The upgrading of females in the Bell system is undoubtedly a source of great satisfaction, as well as financially rewarding, both to the persons involved and to all who support equal opportunity. On the other hand, some costs of this have been assigned by the consent decree to females whose opportunity for jobs have been blocked so that clerical and operator positions may be filled by males.

Employment Distribution by Race and Sex

An excellent statistical picture of changes that have occurred in the race-sex mix of AT&T since the signing of the consent decree is

TABLE III-4

AT&T, Employment by Sex and Occupational Group
1973 and 1979

Occupational Group	Total	1973			
		Male	Percent Male	Female	Percent Female
Officials and Managers	164,438	124,092	75.5	40,346	24.5
Administrative	30,135	5,710	18.9	24,425	81.1
Sales Workers	7,038	4,394	62.4	2,644	37.6
Clerical	207,461	12,254	5.9	195,207	94.1
Operators	143,918	6,425	4.5	137,493	95.5
Total White Collar	552,990	152,875	27.6	400,115	72.4
Outside Crafts	136,391	135,419	99.3	972	0.7
Inside Crafts	97,198	86,757	89.3	10,441	10.7
Service Workers	24,003	18,460	76.9	5,543	23.1
Total Blue Collar	257,592	240,636	93.4	16,956	6.6
Total	810,582	393,511	48.5	417,071	51.5

| | Total | 1979 | | | |
		Male	Percent Male	Female	Percent Female
Officials and Managers	191,436	135,726	70.9	55,710	29.1
Administrative	33,913	8,473	25.0	25,440	75.0
Sales Workers	8,999	4,951	55.0	4,048	45.0
Clerical	231,111	25,626	11.1	205,485	88.9
Operators	102,654	8,068	7.9	94,586	92.1
Total White Collar	568,113	182,844	32.2	385,269	67.8
Outside Crafts	135,072	128,759	95.3	6,313	4.7
Inside Crafts	97,569	80,063	82.1	17,506	17.9
Service Workers	11,098	6,579	59.3	4,519	40.7
Total Blue Collar	243,739	215,401	88.4	28,338	11.6
Total	811,852	398,245	49.1	413,607	50.9

Source: The Company.

provided by Tables III-5 and III-6, which show the percent distribution by occupational group and by race and sex, respectively. In Table III-5, it can be seen that the concentration of blacks in the clerical field has continued even more heavily. In 1979, 43.1 percent of all black employees were clericals as compared with 35.9 percent in 1973. The comparable figures for all employees were 25.6 percent in 1973 and 28.5 percent in 1979. In contrast, the black concentration in the operator classification dropped from 32.4 percent to 20.3 percent and that of all employees from 17.7 percent to 12.6 percent.

These changes result not only from the consent decree but also from changing technology and institutional arrangements. Automatic systems and charges for directory assistance have decimated the operator ranks and increased the use of the clerical function for entry white-collar jobs. Moreover, these and other changes have, in turn, altered the distribution of employees within the company regardless of race or sex. If one looks at the officials and managers group, however, one finds that the percentage of blacks and other minorities in relation to their total percentage in the company has increased more rapidly than the ratio involving all employees. The same situation is found in the administrative and sales categories. Obviously, these changes are products of the consent decree and contribute to the increased proportion of blacks and other minorities who were salaried employees in 1979 as compared with 1973. Meanwhile, the white-collar percentages of all employees remained almost constant.

Given the proportional increases in the black and other minority distribution percentage in white-collar jobs, it is, of course, saying the same thing when one notes that those proportions have declined in the blue-collar area. Significantly, however, both blacks and other minorities reduced their concentration in service work, and blacks raised their share of inside craft activity. Blacks and other minorities, however, fell slightly behind in outside craft work where the competition of females was first being felt.

We emphasize throughout the study that women have been the big gainers from the consent decree, especially if one considers the quantitative aspects. Table III-6 well illustrates this. The proportion of females to the total female population rose by more than one-third in the officials and managers group despite the decline in overall female employment. Females also made slight increases in their proportion in the administrative and sales groups and gained in the clerical area. The decline in operators while males were being introduced into that function and females were being brought into craft jobs resulted in a net decline, albeit a very small one, in the

TABLE III-5

AT&T, Percent Distribution by Race and Occupational Group 1973 and 1979

Occupational Group	1973			1979		
	All Employees	Blacks	Other Minorities	All Employees	Blacks	Other Minorities
Officials and Managers	20.3	5.2	7.6	23.6	11.0	14.0
Administrative	3.7	3.0	2.0	4.2	4.7	3.2
Sales Workers	0.9	0.6	0.7	1.1	1.2	1.0
Clerical	25.6	35.9	37.5	28.5	43.1	39.9
Operators	17.7	32.4	20.1	12.6	20.3	14.6
Total White Collar	68.2	77.1	67.9	70.0	80.3	72.7
Outside Crafts	16.8	9.0	15.3	16.6	8.6	14.7
Inside Crafts	12.0	6.3	11.3	12.0	8.0	10.5
Service Workers	3.0	7.1	5.5	1.4	3.1	2.1
Total Blue Collar	31.8	22.9	32.1	30.0	19.7	27.3
Total	100.0	100.0	100.0	100.0	100.0	100.0

Source: The Company.

TABLE III-6

AT&T, Percent Distribution by Sex and Occupational Group
1973 and 1979

Occupational Group	1973			1979		
	All Employees	Males	Females	All Employees	Males	Females
Officials and Managers	20.3	31.5	9.7	23.6	34.2	13.4
Administrative	3.7	1.5	5.8	4.2	2.1	6.1
Sales Workers	0.9	1.1	0.6	1.1	1.2	1.0
Clerical	25.6	3.1	46.8	28.5	6.4	49.7
Operators	17.7	1.6	33.0	12.6	2.0	22.9
Total White Collar	68.2	38.8	95.9	70.0	45.9	93.1
Outside Crafts	16.8	34.4	0.2	16.6	32.3	1.5
Inside Crafts	12.0	22.1	2.5	12.0	20.1	4.3
Service Workers	3.0	4.7	1.4	1.4	1.7	1.1
Total Blue Collar	31.8	61.2	4.1	30.0	54.1	6.9
Total	100.0	100.0	100.0	100.0	100.0	100.0

Source: The Company.

female white-collar distribution, perhaps an unforeseen result of the consent decree.

In blue-collar jobs, the opening up of inside crafts and the extensive recruiting for outside crafts have increased the distribution of females in these positions, but change is obviously not precipitous.

KEY OCCUPATIONAL GROUPS

The statistics presented above give only skeletal results. We need to examine the occupational groups in greater detail to understand why events unfolded as they did. Then, in a later section, we discuss some key overall impacts of the changing race-sex composition of the AT&T labor force.

Management and Sales Positions

Although total employment in the Bell companies has barely risen since 1973, employment in each of the three top occupational categories—officials and managers, administrative, and sales workers—has increased. In each group, the employment increase was slight, but it has undoubtedly eased somewhat the upgrading of females and minorities.

Nevertheless, changes have clearly been at the expense of white males in two of the three top categories. Thus, in the officials and managers group, the white male participation dropped 7 percent; in the sales category, it declined almost 11 percent. In contrast, administrative positions saw a 4.5 percent increase in the white male share.

Blacks and other minorities, both males and females, improved their participation in each of the three top categories. White females gained as officials and managers and as sales workers but not as administrative employees.

Actually, of course, administrative employees are not top management positions but include lower supervision, executive secretaries, engineering assistants, and special clerks. The fact that females did not gain in these categories is not a failure of affirmative action but, in government EEO enforcement philosophy, a gain. Essentially, as in the case of secretaries and operators, it means that females who held these jobs were upgraded and also that the jobs were open to men. Again, women could have lost opportunities to white males, but a distribution by sex that was approaching "statistical parity" had been achieved.

To emphasize the significance of the changes that have occurred, we examine further the data for key groups beginning with the officials and managers and sales workers categories. The officials and managers group includes not only managerial employees from first-level management to the top but also key professionals such as engineers, scientists, and accountants. These are the positions in which minorities are in exceedingly short supply.[1] Yet, AT&T managed some dramatic percentage (if much smaller actual) increases in the proportion of minorities. Thus, according to Table III-7, between 1973 and 1979, black males in officials and managers positions rose 139.7 percent; Hispanic males, 206.5 percent; and other minority males, 84.1 percent. In contrast, the white male increase was 5.3 percent. Comparable female increases were 135.4 percent for blacks, 188.3 percent for Hispanics, and 117.0 percent for other minorities. White females increased by 28.8 percent, five times the gains of white males, but only about one-fifth that of black females.

White Females—Big Gainers. The largest gainers, however, were white females. Their numbers increased by 10,659 during the consent decree, thereby accounting for almost 40 percent of the increase in total managerial employment. Gains for white females in this category exceeded the combined gains of both black males and females by 4,395 jobs. As one eastern official stated, "It is easier for us to recruit white females to fill job openings than it is to find blacks and other minorities. Almost all employment gains at our company since the consent decree have gone to white females."

Why was this so? Why did white females achieve the strongest gains in this category? The interviews conducted by the authors offered many insights on this point. Of primary importance is the fact that white females, by and large, do not come from the same disadvantaged background as do their counterparts in the remaining protected groups. Belonging to the same economic and social mainstream as white males, they are able to attend the better colleges and universities where the Bell System recruits them from the higher-grade performers. White females thus have a tremendous competitive advantage over other protected group members, and as our results show, they have taken advantage of it.

As one midwestern official commented:

White females have been the ultimate beneficiaries of the consent decree

---

[1] On this point, in general, see Stephen A. Schneider, *The Availability of Minorities and Women for Professional and Managerial Positions 1970–1985,* Manpower and Human Resources Studies No. 7 (Philadelphia: Industrial Research Unit, The Wharton School, University of Pennsylvania, 1977). Questions of availability are also dealt with in a later chapter.

TABLE III-7
AT&T, Labor Force Composition by Race and Sex
Officials and Managers, 1973 and 1979

Race–Sex Group	1973		1979		Percent Change 1973–79
	Number	Percent	Number	Percent	
White Males	120,541	73.3	126,943	66.3	5.3
Black Males	2,167	1.3	5,194	2.7	139.7
Hispanic Males	851	0.5	2,608	1.4	206.5
Other Minority Males	533	0.3	981	0.5	84.1
Total Males	124,092	75.4	135,726	70.9	9.4
White Females	37,054	22.5	47,713	24.9	28.8
Black Females	2,390	1.5	5,627	2.9	135.4
Hispanic Females	579	0.4	1,669	0.9	188.3
Other Minority Females	323	0.2	701	0.4	117.0
Total Females	40,346	24.6	55,710	29.1	38.1
Total	164,438	100.0	191,436	100.0	16.4

Source: The Company.

since they have better qualifications than do minority group employees. Prior to 1973 the thrust of affirmative action at our company was directed toward minorities. Since the consent decree, however, affirmative action has tended to concentrate on white females.

Other protected group members are faced with more difficult circumstances. Although programs to increase minority enrollment have been initiated by the better colleges and universities, most operating companies still find a significant quality differential between the educational backgrounds of white females and those of other members of protected groups. As one official in the southeast commented, "The science and engineering departments of southern black colleges cannot compare with those of VPI, Duke, or Georgia Tech." In addition, as a result of financial exigencies, many minority group members are forced to seek part-time employment while in college, thereby leaving less opportunity for study. Academic achievement suffers as a result.

Finally, it should be noted that white female performance in assessment centers exceeds that of other minority group members. This further increases white female leverage in applying for positions in management. The situation was best expressed by one official who stated, "There is no doubt that white females are adding an additional block to minority improvement." We see these same results in four of the five employment categories selected for detailed study. In sales and craft work as well, white females clearly gained the most ground.

Table III–8 shows comparable data for sales workers. Black and Hispanic males and females showed very substantial percentage gains, and white females, smaller but very significant ones. Other minorities, a very small group, saw their share decline, a result apparently of the failure of American Indians to qualify for or, if qualified, to remain on the job. White males showed a marginal gain of 167 positions, an increase of 4.1 percent; white females were again big gainers.

Thus, in four years, AT&T rather dramatically altered its hiring and promotion patterns for its top-level categories. It accomplished this change and met its targets—again we emphasize that a target which must be met is, beyond question, a quota—in three principal ways: (1) extensive and, undoubtedly, expensively expanded recruiting; (2) upgrading qualified minorities and women; and (3) promoting the "qualified," but not necessarily the "most qualified," who were recruited from a larger population than was formerly the case.

Extensive Recruiting. AT&T's recruiting, like that of other major

TABLE III-8

AT&T, Labor Force Composition by Race and Sex
Sales Workers, 1973 and 1979

Race–Sex Group	1973		1979		Percent Change 1973–79
	Number	Percent	Number	Percent	
White Males	4,032	57.3	4,199	46.7	4.1
Black Males	250	3.5	510	5.7	104.0
Hispanic Males	85	1.2	208	2.3	144.7
Other Minority Males	27	0.4	34	0.4	25.9
Total Males	4,394	62.4	4,951	55.1	12.7
White Females	2,291	32.5	3,144	34.9	37.2
Black Females	251	3.6	705	7.8	180.9
Hispanic Females	67	1.0	167	1.9	149.3
Other Minority Females	35	0.5	32	0.3	-8.6
Total Females	2,644	37.6	4,048	44.9	53.1
Total	7,038	100.0	8,999	100.0	27.9

Source: The Company.

corporations, has been aimed particularly at qualified minorities and women. AT&T has recruited at black colleges and business and engineering schools, selling hard the opportunities available. Both the corporation and affiliated companies have participated. Recruitment in the early 1970s, particularly of engineers, was aided by a precipitous decline in aerospace professional employment and by a recession in other industries while employment of engineers, managers, and sales personnel was growing in the Bell System. This turn of events helped convince potential candidates of the advantages of AT&T employment. Like many corporations, AT&T has been able to "meet the competition." This means paying the going rate to attract appropriately qualified minority or female candidates even if the going rate is highest for them.

Upgrading. As part of its obligations under the consent decree, AT&T made extensive efforts to upgrade minorities and women already on its payrolls. Operating companies' personnel and other management staffs met with all minority and female personnel, encouraged them to apply for higher-rated positions, offered free training, and sincerely and widely "sold" the idea of the new opportunities available. In all cases, employees were both protected against failure and rewarded for success. Those who tried new positions and could not succeed suffered no loss and were guaranteed their former jobs and seniority without break. Financial rewards went to those who succeeded.

Qualified But Not Most Qualified—With a Larger Population. Perhaps the most controversial aspect of the consent decree has been the policy of promoting in order to meet the quotas imposed by the required-to-be-met targets. The Bell System has always prided itself on its careful preparation of managers. Detailed procedures have been developed to evaluate and to test managerial potential in order to obtain, as nearly as possible, the best talent for the job. For example, AT&T developed the new widely used assessment center method of rating and selecting managers.[2]

The consent decree altered managerial selection in two ways. First, it provided a much larger population from which to make the selection. This was particularly the result of opening up the top jobs to women. There is no question about the fact that, prior to the consent decree, AT&T, with considerable variations among operating companies, had been slow to alter traditional, sex-

---

[2] For a discussion of the assessment center approach and an extensive bibliography, see Herbert R. Northrup et al., *The Objective Selection of Supervisors*, Manpower and Human Resources Studies No. 8 (Philadelphia: Industrial Research Unit, The Wharton School, University of Pennsylvania, 1978).

oriented promotion patterns. As a result, many well-qualified women were not permitted to advance in accordance with their potential. In contrast, Bell operating companies had opened their managerial ranks to minorities pursuant to the requirements of Title VII of the Civil Rights Act of 1964 or, in some cases, even before that legislation became effective. The exigencies of the consent decree, however, led to more extensive recruiting and upgrading of minorities and women and therefore also a larger population of these groups.

That these women and minorities offered a greater selection potential for managerial and sales positions than existed before is indisputable. This, of course, has also meant greater competition for white males and, if selection is based wholly on merit, should result in the selection of even more qualified persons than was formerly the rule.

Unfortunately, merit and targets are not compatible objectives, and the targets had to be met. As a result, "qualified but not necessarily the most qualified" persons have received numerous promotions throughout the system. There is no way that we can quantify how often this has occurred, but all personnel executives interviewed testified that it has been both regular and often has been the only way that targets could be met. Thus, the Bell System is setting into place a group of executives, which top officials believe are not the best qualified and which presumably will be charged with running various parts of the system in the years ahead.

The implications of this fact are both difficult to ascertain and potentially staggering. It is, first of all, possible that some of those found "qualified but not the most qualified" are in fact every bit as qualified as those designated most qualified. Selection processes are, of course, at least almost always somewhat subjective. Yet the care with which the Bell System makes selections and the procedures and the number of persons involved all add to the evidence that in the great majority of cases such ratings are quite accurate. Moreover, the pressure to meet the targets—each race plus sex—inevitably must have led to the shading of qualifications so that minorities and females have clearly been given the benefit of the doubt in this regard.

What this will cost in the long run remains to be seen. There is no evidence that the Bell System is running less well today, and it is certainly not less profitable. There were strong indications of adverse morale reactions among white male managers, as is discussed in chapter IV, and this could adversely offset both recruiting and turnover of those who still will provide the majority of future company executives. And, of course, questions of public policy are raised when merit is ignored to right a past wrong at the expense of a person whose only fault is that he is a white male and is presently in competition with a protected group.

Clerical

Government administrators who negotiated the consent decree were, as we have pointed out, as much interested in achieving what they deemed a fair distribution of the AT&T labor force by sex and race as they were in opening up opportunities to women and minorities. So they established targets for white male clericals as they did for women and minorities in more exalted positions. Table III-9 provides convincing evidence that this policy was successful. Thus, white male clericals increased by 110.2 percent between 1973 and 1979, whereas white females declined by 2 percent over the same period. Each category of minority males also expanded very substantially its share of clerical jobs while the comparable minority female group increased its share by a very much smaller ratio. These changes occurred while total clerical employment increased by 23,650, or 11.4 percent.

There are some clerical positions which, like operators' jobs, are appropriate entry positions. No reason in terms of fair public policy can be adduced which would require women, but not men, to start at such positions. Moreover, there are some men who do, or might, prefer clerical positions. No opprobrium should attach to such free choice. Nevertheless, to set required-to-be-met white male targets for these jobs seems questionable. There has been no showing that white males need such "protection" or that males need to replace females as clericals for the public good. One cannot escape the feeling that this part of the consent decree was the result of the personal philosophy of a bureaucratic mind rather than the enforcement of a law.

All operating companies surveyed have made strong attempts to recruit males into this nontraditional form of employment. The main problem encountered in doing this is the lack of clerical and secretarial skills possessed by males. Inquiring into this, one midwestern company found that certain school districts facing budgetary restrictions actively discouraged male students from taking typing and clerical courses. Needless to say, such an approach severely limits the supply of qualified males for clerical positions. Another midwestern company established schools to teach secretarial skills to interested male candidates.

TABLE III-9
AT&T, *Labor Force Composition by Race and Sex*
Clerical, 1973 and 1979

Race–Sex Group	1973		1979		Percent Change 1973–79
	Number	Percent	Number	Percent	
White Males	9,224	4.5	19,386	8.4	110.2
Black Males	1,689	0.8	3,506	1.5	107.6
Hispanic Males	868	0.4	1,988	0.9	129.0
Other Minority Males	473	0.2	746	0.3	57.7
Total Males	12,254	5.9	25,626	11.1	109.1
White Females	155,389	74.9	152,327	65.9	-2.0
Black Females	29,823	14.4	38,927	16.8	30.5
Hispanic Females	7,183	3.5	10,380	4.5	44.5
Other Minority Females	2,812	1.3	3,851	1.7	36.9
Total Females	195,207	94.1	205,485	88.9	5.3
Total	207,461	100.0	231,111	100.0	11.4

Source: The Company.

Why do males desire clerical positions? What makes them seek this nontraditional form of employment? In an affirmative action environment, many males perceive these nontraditional jobs as their only means of entry into nonmanagerial positions at the Bell System. Once having gained entrance, males seek to transfer to craft positions. Such strategic planning was confirmed by several personnel officers surveyed.

Outside Crafts

One of the most interesting and controversial aspects of the consent decree has been the target for outside crafts, which includes line workers and other jobs requiring pole climbing and other physical work. To achieve its targets, AT&T has invested thousands of dollars in special training programs, studies to determine what can be done to improve female performance, recruiting, and last but not least, workers' compensation. AT&T has met its goals, but the costs have been high, particularly in turnover and accidents.

Table III-10 shows the impact of the consent decree quite vividly. Between 1973 and 1979, total employment in outside crafts declined by 1,319, or 1.0 percent, but male employment declined by 6,660, or 4.9 percent. This loss was concentrated among white males, with a 6.3 percent drop; and black males, with only a fraction of the total outside craft employment, with a 2.2 percent decline. Hispanics and other minority males increased their share of work.

The total number of females in outside crafts was not large, but during the five years rose 549.5 percent, with all races sharing in the gain. Blacks and Hispanic females increased their share the most, increasing 1201.8 and 1242.3 percent, respectively. Nevertheless, only 6,313, or 4.7 percent, of the outside craft workers were female in 1979.

To achieve these modest numerical, but astronomical, percentage gains, AT&T has recruited very heavily both inside and outside of the corporation. It should not be surprising that the outside recruiting has been the more successful. Women attracted to clerical or other white-collar positions, like men similarly situated, are not likely also to be attracted to the heavy physical demands of the outside craft work. Those that are so attracted are usually mainly influenced by the potential financial rewards and, to a lesser extent, by the greater opportunity to work without close supervision.

What the Bell System terms the "retreat rates" have been heavy.

TABLE III-10
AT&T, Labor Force Composition by Race and Sex
Outside Crafts, 1973 and 1979

Race–Sex Group	1973		1979		Percent Change 1973–79
	Number	Percent	Number	Percent	
White Males	122,998	90.2	115,275	85.3	-6.3
Black Males	7,848	5.3	7,677	5.7	-2.2
Hispanic Males	3,882	2.9	4,826	3.6	24.3
Other Minority Males	691	0.5	981	0.7	42.0
Total Males	135,419	99.4	128,759	95.3	-4.9
White Females	879	0.6	5,138	3.8	484.5
Black Females	57	0.0	742	0.5	1201.8
Hispanic Females	26	0.0	349	0.3	1242.3
Other Minority Females	10	0.0	84	0.1	740.0
Total Females	972	0.6	6,313	4.7	549.5
Total	136,391	100.0	135,072	100.0	-1.0

Source: The Company.

Physical requirements of the job have discouraged many women; others find pole climbing too difficult or too unpleasant; still others leave the job after finding that the stamina required for the job is either too much in itself or leaves them too fatigued either to enjoy family life or to attend to household duties.

In order to assist females in outside crafts, special pole climbing courses were established by all operating companies. Completion of these courses is now required for all new entrants to outside craft positions regardless of sex. Progression through these courses is on a self-paced basis. Videotaping is provided so that workers can view their performance. Special counselling is available for candidates experiencing difficulty. In spite of this, only one-half the companies surveyed stated that they would initiate a retreat from the school when it became obvious that a worker could not acquire the skills necessary for outside craft work. One company found that 48 percent of all female applicants were unable to complete the pole climbing courses.

Problems continue once the courses have been completed. As one official noted:

> We have a 60 percent dropout and retreat rate for females who successfully complete pole climbing courses. Moreover, we have had some bad accidents involving females in outside crafts. The total accident rate for female outside craftsmen in our company is 22.8 percent, but among men just 10 percent. We had one female employee, a divorcee with two children who badly needed the extra money. She fell off a pole and severely hurt herself.

In addition to pole climbing courses, new safety procedures have been instituted. Equipment has also been modified for female use. Still the accident rates prevail.

Companies deny that they "fragment" outside craft jobs, i.e., break an outside job into a male part and a female part. Some companies, however, do admit assigning females to outside jobs in less strenuous geographical areas. Companies also admit a reluctance to assigning females to outside crafts positions in high crime areas.

Because of the potential for discrimination on the job, we inquired as to whether complaints of harassment had been common. The general consensus was that there had been only a few. Offsetting such evidence were many examples of male chivalry (or perhaps sexist conduct): assignment of females to the less strenuous jobs by supervisors, contrary to management instructions, or assistance by the males so that the females could carry out their duties. The main cause of turnover seems to be that most females are neither physically nor psychologically prepared to handle the job requirements.

Despite all these programs and procedural changes, female turnover in outside craft jobs is extraordinarily high. One southern company reported a retreat rate of 9 percent among males in outside crafts. During this same period of time, the dropout rate for females in these positions was nearly 82 percent. Retreat rates in other areas are in agreement with those cited and cast serious doubts on the ability of AT&T (or anyone else) to alter significantly the male-female balance in outside craft work.

The situation was aptly described by one official who stated, "We have met our female target in outside crafts, but I must be honest and admit that what we have here is a revolving door. It really isn't working out, and the only way we meet our goals is by having a horde of people going in and out."

Accident rates give further, and tragic, proof of the problems of females in outside craft work. Table III-11 shows that females in the introductory outside craft positions have more than twice the accident rate of men and that this situation has continued despite some improvement in the rates for both sexes. Moreover, despite extensive efforts at safety and improved training, including as noted, permitting employees to advance at their own pace, the differential, by sex, in the accident rates has not improved.

There should certainly be no bar to the opportunities for women to work on the lines or in any other jobs. To push sex quotas for such work, however, seems on this evidence as questionable as it does to push those for white male clericals. Certainly, it places governmental EEO philosophy in direct conflict with government support of safety in the work place.

The impact of the sex quotas for clerical and outside craft positions is summarized by the data in Table III 12. In 1973, 17 percent of white male hiring was accounted for by the clerical function and 83 percent by craft work (including outside crafts); but by 1979, 43.7 percent of all white male hiring was for clerical work and 56.3 percent for the crafts. Obviously, the insistence on hiring commensurate with parity objectives for the labor force was pursued regardless of turnover, costs, injuries, and most likely of applicant desires as well.

In recognition of the obvious difficulties caused by the accelerated placement and advancement of females in outside crafts, AT&T has decided to retrench from its initial objectives. Under the consent decree, the Bell System had set an ultimate share of 19 percent for females in outside craft positions. Upon termination of

TABLE III-11
AT&T, Accident Rates per 1,000 Workers
Introductory Outside Crafts, 1973–77

	1973	1977
Bell System	12.38	10.26
Males	12.22	9.79
Females	29.14	26.73

Source: The Company.

TABLE III-12
AT&T, Percent Introductory White Male Hiring
Clerical and Crafts, 1973–79

	1973	1979
Clerical	17.0	43.7
Crafts	83.0	56.3

Source: The Company.

the decree, the share was lowered to 9 percent, which the company considers to be a more realistic figure. This reduction should have the further benefit of reducing turnover and accident rates in these positions.

Inside Crafts

In contrast to outside craft work, women are coming into the inside craft positions and working out well. Table III-13 shows that despite a 0.4 percent drop in total employment—virtually all at the expense of white males—female employment in this category rose by 67.7 percent, and minority female employment rose by a considerably larger percentage. Gains were also made by black and Hispanic males.

Inside craft work includes "framing," which is essentially electrical and electronic assembling. In manufacturing companies—including Western Electric Company, the Bell System's manufacturing arm—this work has been overwhelmingly female, at least since World War II. Nevertheless, prior to the consent decree, the Bell System had largely institutionalized earlier hiring patterns and looked upon this as a "male job."[3] The ease with which women are

---

[3] The tendency of companies—often with union concurrence and/or insistence—to institutionalize the hiring patterns of the era when the operation either began or matured was long a factor in employment patterns and, of course, a principal target of Title VII of the Civil Rights Act of 1964. See Herbert R. Northrup et al., *Negro Employment in Basic Industry,* Studies of Negro Employment Vol. I (Philadelphia: Industrial Research Unit, The Wharton School, University of Pennsylvania, 1970), especially Parts One and Eight.

TABLE III-13

AT&T, Labor Force Composition by Race and Sex
Inside Crafts, 1973 and 1979

Race–Sex Group	1973		1979		Percent Change 1973–79
	Number	Percent	Number	Percent	
White Males	78,828	81.1	71,182	73.0	-9.7
Black Males	4,841	5.0	5,499	5.6	13.6
Hispanic Males	2,236	2.3	2,521	2.6	12.7
Other Minority Males	852	0.8	861	0.9	1.1
Total Males	86,757	89.2	80,063	82.1	-7.7
White Females	8,957	9.2	14,015	14.3	56.5
Black Females	1,140	1.2	2,419	2.5	112.2
Hispanic Females	261	0.3	792	0.8	203.4
Other Minority Females	83	0.1	280	0.3	237.3
Total Females	10,441	10.8	17,506	17.9	67.7
Total	97,198	100.0	97,569	100.0	0.4

Source: The Company.

working into these jobs is proof of the inappropriateness of the System's former policy.

Inside crafts also include building maintenance, and here women are progressing much more slowly. Many, as in outside crafts, find the jobs too strenuous. Others lack the training and skills for such jobs as operating steam equipment, plumbing, carpentry, or electrical work. Progress in obtaining females for these jobs has been slow and beset with heavy turnover and obviously high recruiting costs.

CONCLUDING REMARKS

The consent decree has clearly increased the opportunities for females and minorities at the expense of white males. It has, however, also exhibited what we believe is an overconcern toward parity employment in such positions as clerical and outside crafts where greater concentration on minority needs might well better serve the public interest.

CHAPTER IV

Organizational Impact

The consent decree caused some radical shifts in the manner in which the Bell System handled its employee relations. Some of the impact of these changes has been alluded to or commented upon in chapter III. In this chapter, we consider the implications of the implementation of the decree on quality of the labor force, organizational structure, the role of the supervisor, discipline, employee attitudes, and union relations.

QUALITY OF THE LABOR FORCE

In the rush to increase the representation of protected group members, many companies reported initial declines in quality of the labor force. These declines were particularly noticeable in urban areas. As an official of an eastern operating company stated, "More workers from disadvantaged backgrounds are being hired than ever before. Since the late sixties, we have noticed a significant decline in the quality of the urban labor force."

Although the operating companies have more recently been making a strenuous effort to cull out substandard performers, this has not been entirely successful. First of all, it is complicated by the need to meet the consent decree's employment targets. Our impression is that when rejection of the person jeopardizes quota fulfillment, performance that is marginal or even slightly less can be considered passable. Moreover, as we discuss below, many supervisors have become overly cautious in the rating or disciplining of protected groups. Consequently, some substandard performers are allowed to remain on the job.

In the heavily Hispanic areas, language difficulties compounded by a determination to maintain Spanish as the employee's first language accentuate the problem. One can appreciate the desire of Hispanic groups to preserve their customs and language. Nevertheless, their drive for bilingualism tends both to shut them off from the non-Spanish speaking majority and to reduce their proficiency in English, the language of the majority and of business. Because verbal communication is what the telephone is all about, those less proficient in English can reduce both their own capability and the quality of performance of the telephone operating organization.

In urban centers, users of the telephone have experienced operators whose language comprehension, verbal understanding, or pronunciation are poor or weak. These problems are reduced by the increasing substitution of equipment for operators, but they do indeed persist in other employee groups. Part of the problem may be the deteriorating quality of education and the labor force associated with decaying urban areas, but at the very least, the need to meet employment targets compounds a situation over which the Bell System has little control.

Finally, note should be made of the impact of forcing men through clerical channels and of encouraging women into outside crafts. Both situations encourage rapid turnover and thereby increase the number and proportion of learners and less-experienced personnel on the job at any given time. This can only reduce productivity. Moreover, whenever an accident occurs, work is interrupted and productivity lessened. The high accident rates for females in outside crafts thus also reduces efficiency.

More Talent v. Not Promoting the "Most Qualified"

As a result of the consent decree, the pool of workers considered for promotions has been dramatically increased. Attention has been called to qualified minorities, and large numbers of women have had opportunities opened to them. Many of these candidates, particularly in the management and marketing areas, are extremely able and ambitious. Obviously, this has the potential of enhancing the quality of labor.

In addition, the personnel departments, under the close monitoring of AT&T's central office, now play a much greater role in promotions and upgrading. This has the potential of lending greater objectivity to the process by making it more difficult for supervisors to ignore strong candidates in favor of friends or associates.

Third, one of the by-products of the decree has been an added emphasis on training and career planning within the Bell System. Job qualifications and career advancement paths are more clearly defined than before. This has helped improve the caliber of workers promoted by operating companies.

These positive factors, unfortunately, may well be overbalanced by a number of serious negative ones. Even though personnel officials of operating companies enthusiastically describe the intelligence and capabilities of the newly promoted female managers, at the same time, they lament these managers' lack of experience and the fact that efficiency has been seriously retarded by inadequate training. Such talented people have been promoted over the heads of more experienced, more mature, and better-trained personnel in order to meet targets. Both the careers of people thus promoted and the quality of work would obviously be enhanced by upward movement which first provided more experience in the job below.

One operating company reported that it had promoted to key managerial positions minorities and women who had very little experience. This is not believed to be unusual. Such rapid upward movement deprives the person promoted of the broad base of exposure necessary for effective performance in a job for which individual judgment, grounded in experience, is often the most crucial factor in successful decision making. Moreover, particularly in a quota environment, the lack of experience reduces the manager's credibility vis-à-vis his older, more-senior subordinates, and this, in turn, also reduces managerial effectiveness.

The extended implication of selecting the "basically qualified" as opposed to the most-qualified candidates has yet to be realized. Will the truly outstanding performers continue to sit back while basically qualified workers receive the promotions? (This problem is compounded in situations for which the standards necessary to be basically qualified are lowered in order to achieve targets.) What kind of long-run performance can be expected from people who know that outstanding achievement may not be as important an input in their advancement as their sex or the color of their skin? Also, will new, aspiring workers want to join a corporation where performance is not always rewarded? We believe that, at the very least, Bell System managers who are passed over in order to allow targets to be met will tend to seek retirement as early as possible in order to find opportunities elsewhere. Only time will demonstrate the impact of such developments.

One such impact is already becoming increasingly apparent to the Bell System operating companies. As outlined in chapter II, the modern telecommunications industry is characterized by extensive competition (particularly between AT&T and IBM in the area of data systems) with its concurrent demands for greater operational efficiency. This requirement for increased productivity would seem to be at cross-purposes with the promotion standard of basically qualified instead of most qualified.

The failure to promote the most-qualified personnel can be particularly felt by supervisors and lower-level managers on whom increasing demands are being placed to improve productivity with a less than maximum quality labor force. As noted in a recent business periodical:

> It appears that the most severe pressures are occurring along the fault line that divides low-level supervisors and workers in the field.
> This division has intensified in the last 10 years, as the Bell monopoly began to meet growing competition at many levels of its business. AT&T's mammoth reorganization last fall, coupled with the continuing introduction of new technology in the highly automated Bell System, has put enormous downward pressure on supervisors and workers to increase productivity.[1]

It is not difficult to understand that the actions in support of the consent decree conflict with its stress on increased productivity brought about by the rapidly advancing competitive environment of the industry. This in turn may well add to greater employee resentment both among protected and nonprotected workers.

Although the enhanced role of the staff personnel officers in the promotion process can and, in the long run, might well bring greater objectivity and scope to selections, it has not necessarily worked totally in that direction. Even though supervisors must now provide greater support and evidence for their recommendations, the personnel officers are primarily concerned with achieving the targets of the consent decree. Hence, their pressure is certainly not concentrated on achieving more quality but rather on finding someone who is qualified *and* can meet the race or sex requirements needed. As long as this is true, the greater objectivity theorized by staff personnel involvement—and, indeed, often control—of the promotion process would seem to be unrealizable.

ORGANIZATIONAL STRUCTURE

The consent decree caused the Bell System to expand considerably its staff of personnel specialists involved in equal employment opportunity (EEO) and related work. At the corporate level, the employee relations function was divided and a second corporate officer was appointed. Manpower, including EEO, activities are assigned to one officer and labor relations and related work to the other. Each operating company and major segment therein now have key personnel assigned to EEO duties, monitoring, and enforcement.

---

[1] "The Dissatisfaction at AT&T," *Business Week,* June 25, 1979, p. 91.

The Bell System has been careful not to make EEO tasks a minority or female job. Protected group personnel are not excluded from these tasks; however, the key jobs in this area have generally been assigned either to experienced personnel whose appointment gives a clear indication to all employees of the company's commitment in achieving its targets or to an obviously upward-moving younger manager for whom promotions are expected as a consequence of achieving results.

Centralization

It is not extended staffs, however, but degree of control that has been the greatest impact of the consent decree on the Bell System organization. Whenever an organization is threatened with harm by an outside force, it centralizes to protect itself. Thus, even in decentralized companies, union relations must be subject to careful corporate scrutiny and control. To do otherwise would, for example, permit a plant manager to set overall company wage policy by agreeing to a settlement that could spread through the company at great cost. Typically, the local management is "advised" by the corporate staff on labor relations. Sophisticated students of management and industrial relations understand that local management rejects this "advice" at its peril.

EEO and health and safety government regulations have had similar effects. Violation of such regulations or even failure to affirmatively pursue government directed objectives in these fields can cost a concern great direct financial loss, possible customer rejection, and bad publicity. Hence, centralization has again occurred with corporate staff "advice" in effect becoming policy from which little dissension is permitted and with line officials rated on their performance in these areas.

Hiring and Promotion Process

By its very nature, the effective pursuit of targets necessitates a centralization of authority within the personnel office. The Bell System is faced with the task of achieving various employment targets (allocation rates) by race-sex group within each job classification. The purpose of the targets is to make the AT&T labor force more accurately reflect the underlying employment and labor force.

With the attainment of these allocation rates as the top priority under the consent decree, it is only logical to expect the control of the personnel office to extend to the lowest possible level. Gone are the days when operating divisions could hire and promote on their own authority. The achievement of quotas is too important to be left to varying interpretations at the local operating level.

The personnel office, by using the output of the GOALS 2 program, establishes the yearly employment targets. In addition, the office monitors the various operating divisions to insure that targets are being met. Several personnel officers surveyed viewed their function, in part, as that of a policeman or of an internal auditor with respect to achieving targets.

One effective way to insure that targets are met is by following a "packaging" system. Under such an approach, if a target cannot be met, all succeeding promotions are held up until the opening is filled by a candidate with the appropriate race-sex mix. Then all remaining promotions can be filled as a package. Logjams of this type occur most often in the crucial area of management. One company held up twenty promotions to top-level management in 1977 in order to fill a target.

In addition to the packaging concept, the personnel office has also acquired veto power over promotions and hires in cases where targets must be achieved. For example, some operating companies utilize assessment centers as part of the management selection process. All companies using such centers reported significantly lower average performance on the part of minority group members. In all cases, where targets had to be met, the results of the assessment center evaluation were subordinated to the attainment of allocation rates.

Two other areas graphically demonstrate the overwhelming priority given to meeting race-sex targets. A traditional goal in personnel selection and advancement has always been the choice of the best-qualified person for the job. This principle has been widely violated, but even when it was being abrogated, it still remained an openly acknowledged objective.

As already noted, being the best qualified is no longer insurance of promotion. All personnel officials interviewed by the authors acknowledged that the selection of the best-qualified worker no longer applies as a meaningful goal. It has been replaced by selection of a "basically qualified" individual of the proper race-sex mix. When a target must be met, selection of a worker of the required race and sex takes priority over all other qualifications.

As one eastern official stated, "The emphasis here is on the selection of 'qualified' as opposed to the 'most-qualified' personnel. However, given several qualified personnel in the required race-sex category, the most qualified of these workers will be selected for advancement."

The problem has been compounded in that the definition of "basically qualified" has been lowered in order to achieve targets. One midwestern official noted, "A basic battery of tests must be passed in order to be employed by our company. Occasionally, minimum test requirements have been lowered to insure that targets are met."

Another time-honored criterion for selection, especially in supervisory and managerial positions, has been a time-in-grade requirement. The implication here is that senior supervisory and managerial positions demand sufficient levels of experience for optimum performance. This principle has also been overturned when the need for filling a target arises. Given several candidates of the appropriate race-sex mix, experience will be a deciding factor; if only one candidate filling the required race-sex attributes is available, however, experience is no longer an operative qualification. Many of the personnel officials expressed severe doubts about the validity of this procedure.

Typical of this attitude was the statement by one vice-president. "A major problem at our company has been the accelerated promotion of inexperienced managers in order to achieve targets. Some blacks and females have been promoted to middle-level management with less than six months of managerial experience. Quotas occasionally take precedence over time-in-grade requirements for managerial promotion."

With targets that must be met, centralization was thus inevitably enhanced in the Bell System. Not only have staff personnel officers had their authority over personnel selection, hiring, promotion, and discipline greatly increased to the point where they have, in many cases, the final determination, but the corporate personnel staff now also monitors the entire process of fulfilling the company's obligations under the decree. The effect, of course, is a significant diminution of line authority from first-line supervisor on up.

THE ROLE OF THE SUPERVISOR

Supervision, particularly at the lower levels, has been directly affected by the consent decree. With their job content, authority, and responsibility dramatically altered, many supervisors, especially older ones, have found it difficult to adjust to this redefinition of their role within the Bell System.

Consider first the supervisor's control over his subordinates. Prior to the consent decree, many supervisors held authority for initial hiring into their divisions. Now, under the expanded control of the hiring and promotion process exerted by the personnel office, this authority has been stripped from the supervisor. Supervisors, in turn, regard this as a loss of control over those who work for them. Supervisors are held accountable for the results of their subordinates, but they can no longer determine who these subordinates will be. Many senior supervisors, schooled under the previous system, express dissatisfaction with the new approach.

The role of the supervisor in the promotion process has also been drastically curtailed. Prior to the advent of affirmative action, many supervisors controlled the advancements of those within their divisions. Clearly, the power to regulate the progress of subordinates greatly increased the authority and control that the supervisor was able to exert over those reporting to him.

Again, as with initial hires, this prerogative has been relegated to the personnel office. Although recommendations of supervisors are considered an input to the promotion decision, they are not the sine qua non. Supervisors, quite correctly, regard this loss of control over the advancement paths of their subordinates as a diminution of their authority and stature within the Bell System. As one midwestern official noted, "Supervisors view affirmative action as a direct control exerted by the personnel office over the employee selection process. Previously, supervisors had control over promotions and hiring. They no longer do so, and they deeply resent this."

Some operating companies, in recognizing this dilemma, have encouraged supervisors to nominate for promotion only those workers of the proper race-sex mix. This is done in an attempt to spare the supervisor the obvious embarrassment of having his recommendation disregarded when attainment of a target takes priority. Even if embarrassment is avoided, however, the basic issue remains—supervisors have lost the ability to promote whomever they want. This loss of leverage vis-à-vis their subordinates must significantly reduce supervisory authority.

In the redefined world of targets, many supervisors find themselves at a loss. Several of those interviewed noted a reluctance on the part of supervisors to take disciplinary action against protected group workers. Many supervisors were also hesitant about writing bad evaluations for these workers. Supervisors were characterized as "running scared" and concerned about covering themselves with sufficient documentation when disciplining protected group members.

As we discuss later, protected groups have a whole new system available to them for seeking redress of complaints. Essentially, this means that grievances or complaints can be taken up without going through regular organizational hierarchies and without involving the union bargaining agent even if union-represented employees are involved. Under this complaint procedure, the affected employee usually takes the problem to an EEO counsellor. Minorities in particular have been found to utilize this extrahierarchical procedure.

Whatever the benefits of the extrahierarchical complaint procedure, its very existence tends to subvert supervisory authority. It also encourages supervisors to avoid decisions, such as disciplinary actions, that might involve complaints and, at the very least, that require detailed justifications of their actions to counsellors and to higher company officials.

Supervisors manifest an ambivalent attitude toward the EEO counsellors created by some companies. On the one hand, supervisors regard them as being a source of advice on how to deal effectively with protected group workers. On the other hand, however, they see quite clearly that the "open-door" policies of the counsellors (and of higher-level management) subvert the chain of command and reduce their authority. Yet, they are still charged with the responsibilities for job performance of their subordinates whom they can no longer hire, promote, or as they see it, discipline.

The final problem for supervisors arises from training requirements. Traditionally, supervisors have provided on-the-job training for their subordinates, and this requirement has often been ignored or at least given low priority. It is a fact of industrial life that training is always the first thing sacrificed when operational demands arise. Under affirmative action, however, there is a need for wider pools of adequately trained protected group workers. This, in turn, places an added burden on the supervisor, who must insure that this training is accomplished. Supervisors, now held accountable for developing their subordinates, regard this requirement as something extra to be accomplished in addition to their normal duties, especially when the subordinates are not of their choosing and cannot be rewarded as the supervisor would direct.

In short, the supervisor views his job requirements as being expanded at the same time that his personal authority has been curtailed. Traditional supervisory control of hiring and promotions has been eliminated or at least drastically reduced. Without these time-honored checks on their subordinates, many supervisors are finding it difficult to accomplish their job. Open-door policies of upper-level management and affirmative action counsellors constitute a diversion of the chain of command in the eyes of the supervisors, and they are certainly finding it difficult to adjust to their redefined role within the Bell System.

The situation was aptly described by one midwestern official who noted: "Supervisors regard EEO as an additional burden. Moreover, although they understand that the company is committed and they know they have to do it, they regard it as an unfair burden as well."

Diminished authority with more responsibility is, of course, a way of life for supervisors in many companies. The shift at Bell, however, has been radical and could cause the company severe problems in the long run. It would certainly not be surprising under the circumstances to find that Bell System supervisors were attempting to develop an organizational approach to this problem so that their voice could be heard when decisions are made that affect their responsibility and authority.

DISCIPLINE

Despite energetic attempts by top officials to prevent it, a double standard of performance and discipline has arisen. Failure to perform or to conduct oneself according to rules and regulations is simply overlooked by some supervisors in order to avoid either being overruled or dragged through inquiries which the supervisor may find onerous. Moreover, if the supervisor "wins" the case, then a replacement must compensate for the loss of a protected group member. Because targets must be met, the supervisor may well be forced to accept a replacement of someone else's choosing. It would be surprising if the attitude of "why bother" did not become prevalent.

Supervisors' reluctance to take action against protected group members has resulted in senior personnel officials becoming more involved in the disciplinary process. One eastern vice-president stated that he had found it necessary to publicly support his supervisors in discipline cases. A midwestern official noted, "Supervisors are now consulting more often with top personnel officials in discipline matters concerning protected group members." This, of course, may present reversals of supervisory action. It is also, however, one more indication of diluted supervisory control and of the care with which protected groups are handled.

A personnel executive of an operating company put it this way:

> Supervisors handle protected groups as they do union shop stewards. If they cannot document the action down to the head of a pin, they do not pursue the matter. But this analogy only goes so far. It is far easier to

deal with the union over a problem than it is with the government or our management determined to meet targets despite declining employment. More and more supervisors are being convinced that they better just endure problems and forget about discipline.

In the significant areas of absenteeism and tardiness, Bell System personnel seem to have the situation under control. One reason, of course, is that infractions of such rules are objectively ascertained and can be easily defended. Even here, however, affirmative action counsellors were used to supplement regular training programs and the activities of supervision. Although a problem in the early days of the consent decree, most operating companies now report that the absentee rates are about the same as before the decree was instituted.

In this regard, one eastern operating company vice-president noted: "Absenteeism and discipline problems occurred initially among newly recruited minority workers. We attributed a large part of this to a history of 'day work' among the newly hired employees. The institution of training programs for both new employees and supervisors has significantly reduced these problems." Because the Bell System is a public utility charged with providing service twenty-four hours a day and 365 days a year, it has always exercised a rigorous control of absentees and tardiness, and it has obviously continued to do so during the consent decree period.

EMPLOYEE ATTITUDES

It appears obvious that there must be considerable differences among Bell employees in regard to the implementation of the consent decree. All personnel officials confirmed that white male employees overwhelmingly regard it as an unfair burden, and minorities and women generally approve of it. Minorities believe— and the evidence in chapter III supports this—that women are the principal beneficiaries of the decree.

The Bell System companies survey their employees on many questions. Although we did not find that most company survey data provided discerning questions in regard to employee attitudes, what information exists and what we were able to discuss all indicate some serious morale problems for the white male employees. Bell System management has attempted to counter this by emphasizing that the consent decree was essential to the company's growth and prosperity and that it represents the law of the land. The emphasis on the legality of the programs required by the consent decree has been significant in gaining worker acceptance for the new hiring and promotion policies formulated to attain necessary utilization rates, but problems still exist with regard to worker attitudes.

Our statistical analysis has shown that white males have experienced reduced opportunities in four of the five employment categories examined. As one eastern official stated, "Some white males at our company would need four hundred years of seniority to get promoted in 1977." Although this may be somewhat of an exaggeration, it clearly has strong implications for worker attitudes. As might be expected, all interviews conducted noted that most white males have been extremely antagonistic toward affirmative action. For example, in a 1978 attitudinal survey by AT&T, 25 percent of nonmanagement employees agreed with the statement that "the best and brightest white males will have left the Bell System."[2] The following comments reflect this position:

EEO in theory is best for everyone, but not so in real life . . . .
The widespread practice of reverse discrimination to meet [affirmative action] goals is the major cause of poor morale in my building. . . .
One thing that really bothers me is moving up in the company. I am white, male, 25. I am not a brain, but average. I have a lot of drive and want to get ahead. I have just been notified there is some kind of freeze which will last 3 or 4 months. In that time, if I am passed over, the company will go to the street. This is not fair. I work for the company but my chances are less than someone on the street.[3]

In addition to the general attitudinal problems resulting from reduced opportunities and the increasingly competitive environment prevailing in the telecommunications industry, other difficulties have arisen. For example, white males are deeply resentful of the cash payments that were part of the settlement of the consent decree made to protected group workers. This liberality toward a segment is used by the unions as a sort of company favoritism and as a further need for wage adjustments to bargaining unit employees.

White males also express resentment over female gains in the supervisory and managerial positions. One midwestern official commented, "White males resent women getting the high paying jobs. Their opinion is that these jobs should go to 'breadwinners.' "

Two interesting contrasts in white male attitudes were noted in our interviews. Many companies reported morale problems among white males in situations where they were subordinate to a female. These same companies reported no major attitudinal problems

2 AT&T, "Bell System Employee Communications Study, 1978 Results. Detailed Findings Report-2," p. 38.
3 *Ibid.*, p. 35.

among white males when they were subordinate to males from other minority groups. This can possibly be explained by the military background of many of the white males. In the service, they were often supervised by members of other racial and ethnic groups.

Second, attitudes toward affirmative action among white males are said to deteriorate as age increases. Younger workers are less disturbed by targets than are older workers. This fact was noted in all interviews conducted by the authors.

Morale problems encountered by protected group workers normally arise from what they perceive to be the slow pace of affirmative action. Several companies report the formation of pressure groups by blacks and females to speed implementation of the decree. This impatience is especially evident among minority personnel. For example, attitudinal surveys reveal marked discrepancies in white and nonwhite perceptions of how well and how fast the consent decree is changing these. Table IV-1 illustrates that whites in a key northern operating company consider that the decree programs will be much more effective than do nonwhites with respect to target attainment. Whites in this company also rate company compliance with EEO guidelines at a higher level than do nonwhites.

Differences in attitudes toward the consent decree also exist among management and nonmanagement personnel. As set forth in Table IV-2, a company in the south noted the percentage of employ ees who gave "unsatisfactory" replies to key questions concerning consent decree issues.

The social change compelled by the consent decree was certain to have initiated considerable resentment, particularly by those who were hurt through no fault of their own but also by those who felt that they were not assisted enough. It seems also certain to exacerbate divisions among races and sexes. The surprise, perhaps, is not that it has adversely affected attitudes, but that there is so little impact discernible. Again, the question is how the impact will be over time, and here, only time will provide the answer.

In all fairness it should be noted that, in response to the increasingly competitive environment of the telecommunications industry, AT&T has recently begun a sweeping reorganization. The structural and operational changes thus initiated and the company's necessary heavy emphasis on productivity have contributed to increased worker stress and declines in morale—some of which may be reflected in the above quotations.[4]

---

[4] "Coping with Anxiety at AT&T," *Business Week*, May 28, 1979, p. 95; "The Dissatisfaction at AT&T," p. 91.

TABLE IV-1

Northern Bell System Operating Company
Percentage of Employees Agreeing with Selected
Attitude Survey Questions, by Race, 1977

Statement	Whites	Nonwhites
All or most of the EEO targets will be met.	73	31
Management performance has been adequate in complying with EEO regulations.	78	46

Source: The Bell Operating Company.

TABLE IV-2

Bell Operating Company in South
Percentage of "Unsatisfactory" Replies Given to
Consent Decree-Related Questions, 1977

Question	Management	Nonmanagement
How well do you understand the EEO program?	4.4	20.8
Do you agree with the goals of the affirmative action program?	59.7	67.1
Does the company make every effort to provide equal employment opportunity to all workers?	39.1	54.2

Source: The Bell Operating Company.

It would be unwise, however, to assign sole responsibility to organizational change for this decline in worker attitudes. As Tables IV-1 and IV-2 indicate, significant problems existed more than a year before AT&T began its reorganization, and it is very likely that whatever the reorganization problems, they have been compounded by the consent decree experience. Clearly, then, the consent decree has been a major factor in the reduction in morale among Bell System employees.

UNION RELATIONS

The consent decree posed difficult questions for unions representing Bell System employees. The affirmative action override in effect set aside a cardinal union principle—seniority. In fact, the override abrogated sections of the contracts between Bell System companies and various unions. This gave the unions little choice other than to attack the decree by all legal means. This they did through grievance machinery, arbitrations, and court cases. The company denied the grievances and refused to put into effect arbitrators' decisions where the arbitrators decided that the contracts, not the consent decree, were paramount—which occurred in about one-half of the several arbitrations involving this issue. Then, as noted in chapter I, the courts settled the issue in favor of the primacy of the consent decree.

In moving against the consent decree, the unions were on the horns of a dilemma. The course that they followed obviously alienated the minorities and females who were profiting by the decree. If they did not, they would have alienated their dominant group, white males, and run counter to traditional union policy as well. Perhaps they came out as well as possible; they fought for principle (and their majority constituency) but lost, thereby not irrevocably losing their minority and female support.[5]

In all the regions that we visited, union leadership is dominantly white male. The Communications Workers of America (CWA) has made a valiant attempt to increase its female and minority staff and has had more success with the former than the latter. The International Brotherhood of Electrical Workers (IBEW), coming as it does from a strong construction industry with an exclusionist background, and the independent unions seem to work less at integration.

The unions have also incurred problems at the local level as a result of the consent decree. We found that minorities with grievances depended very little on the union assistance. Instead they took the alternate, extrahierarchical route, either through EEO counsellors or through filing charges with the EEOC or state or local agencies. Women tended to favor this latter route also, but not by so overwhelming a percentage, and also did not file nearly as many cases. Thus, although the unions remain exclusive bargaining agents, they have lost control of the issues and of the support of a constituency. Instead, these issues and this constituency use agencies of the government or a service provided by the company as a result of government action. It remains to be seen how this development will affect union relations in the years ahead and

---

[5] In an interesting case, the IBEW sued New Jersey Bell to enforce an arbitration which ordered the company to give a clerical job to a high-seniority female instead of a low-seniority male. The male was given the job to fill a quota. The company refused to act on the arbitrator's award, and the U.S. Court of Appeals supported its position on grounds that the consent decree was paramount. *IBEW Local 827, Telephone Workers v. New Jersey Bell Telephone Co.*, 577 F.2d 368 (1968).

whether it will continue now that the consent decree is no longer in effect.

CONCLUDING REMARKS

The discussion in this chapter has dealt with various qualitative impacts of the consent decree. Although supporting data cannot be objectively presented, these aspects may well be the most significant and could alter how the Bell System works and what it achieves.

CHAPTER V

Regional Variations

In this chapter, the focus of the analysis shifts from the national to the regional level. By examining regional differences in utilization of race-sex groups, we can consider such questions as the effect of labor supply on the composition of the work force and, more importantly, the tradeoffs between various protected groups. Cultural and educational differences and their effects on the labor supply process can also be discussed when examining the data at the regional level.

Other questions which were of paramount importance at the national level recede into the background. Thus, for example, our interviews noted no regional differences in discipline, employee attitudes, the role of the supervisor, the impact of technology, and union relations.

METHODOLOGY

Using the U.S. Bureau of the Census definitions, we have segregated the AT&T employment data by region, occupation, race, and sex (see Table V-1). These data are set forth in Appendix V-A. In regions in which Hispanics or other minority groups exceed one percent of the total, they are set forth in separate columns; otherwise they are combined.

In general, the regional data follow the national pattern, but there are significant variations. We therefore first consider the regions where race-sex groups made significant progress. The converse question is also considered. Not surprisingly, in a system geared to the achievement of statistical parity, we find that the extent of the progress attained by a protected group is determined by that group's relative labor supply. Thus Hispanics, for example, achieved their largest gains in the West and the Southwest because this is where they constitute a relatively significant segment of the population.

This leads directly into our second question: the tradeoffs between race-sex groups. If we find that Hispanics achieved significant

TABLE V-1
Regional Definitions

Region	States
New England	Maine, Vermont, New Hampshire, Massachusetts, Connecticut, Rhode Island
Middle Atlantic	New York, New Jersey, Pennsylvania
South Atlantic	Delaware, Maryland, Washington, D.C., West Virginia, Virginia, North Carolina, South Carolina, Georgia, Florida
East North Central	Ohio, Indiana, Illinois, Michigan, Wisconsin
East South Central	Kentucky, Tennessee, Alabama, Mississippi
West North Central	Minnesota, Iowa, Missouri, Kansas, Nebraska, South Dakota, North Dakota
West South Central	Arkansas, Oklahoma, Louisiana, Texas
Mountain	Montana, Wyoming, Colorado, New Mexico, Idaho, Utah, Arizona, Nevada
Pacific	California, Oregon, Washington, Alaska, Hawaii

Source: U.S., Department of Commerce, Social and Economic Statistics Administration, Bureau of the Census, *1970 Census of the Population* (Washington, D.C.: U.S. Government Printing Office).

representational progress in the West, what can we say of blacks in the same region? If black gains are minimal (where "minimal" has been suitably defined), then Hispanics substitute for blacks in this region. When aggregated across all nine regions, behavior of this type will be termed a tradeoff between the race-sex groups involved.

The analysis of the labor supply process and tradeoffs was conducted for each of the five key employment categories previously analyzed in chapter III. The regional results are presented by these categories. In addition to discussing the labor supply process and tradeoffs, any significant regional differences that affect operational performance are also noted. Primary among these are regional differences in accident rates in outside craft positions.

Development of a Metric

Statistical tables in chapter III show the percentage composition of the AT&T labor force by race-sex groups for the years 1973 and 1979. For example, in management, black males accounted for 1.3 percent of all positions in 1973. In 1979, they had increased their representation to 2.7 percent in this job category. The differential of 1.4 percent (2.7 percent–1.3 percent) is thus the nationwide gain experienced by black males in this occupational classification during this time period.

This nationwide advance, however, is the weighted sum of the individual advances experienced by black males in the nine regions into which we have disaggregated the national data. The logical extension of this is the following metric: When a specific race-sex group achieves a regional gain which exceeds its nationwide advance, we say that a *substantial gain* has occurred. All substantial gains refer to changes in percentage representation within an individual job category.

Consider again the case of black males in management. In each of the nine regions, black managerial representation increased between 1973 and 1979. Yet, the tables in Appendix V-A reveal that in only three of the nine regions (South Atlantic, East South Central, and West South Central) did black male gains exceed the nationwide advance of 1.4 percent. Using our metric, we say that only in these three regions did black managers achieve substantial gains.

Covariance

A corollary of this approach is used for analyzing tradeoffs. Suppose we were to compare the substantial gains of black males with those of white females for each of these nine regions in the officials and managers category. Were we to do this, we would find that, in six of the nine regions, substantial gains by one group were accompanied by gains for the other group that were less than that group's nationwide advance.

We term a situation of this type evidence of a tradeoff between the race-sex groups involved. In other words, within a given occupational classification, when substantial advances by one group are accompanied by minimal gains (i.e., gains less than the nationwide average) on the part of a second group, the two can be viewed as competing against each other for the fixed number of positions available. It is this form of competition that will be termed a tradeoff.

The statistical parameter used to compare representational gains by two different parties is termed covariance. A negative covariance will be evidence of a tradeoff between the groups involved. A positive covariance will signify that the two groups complement each other. A heuristic discussion of the concept of covariance is included in Appendix V-B.

ANALYSIS OF REGIONAL DATA

Using the five key employment categories examined in detail in chapter III and the regional data as presented in the tables in

Appendix V-A, an analysis of the gains in minority group representation was conducted. Attempts were made to explain these representational gains using such economic variables as employment changes, earnings growth, growth in plant and equipment, and growth in total assets. None of these measures provided a significant explanation of the regional differences in minority representation, as developed in Appendix V-C.

Economic variables thus did not explain regional differences. This should not be surprising when one acknowledges that the purpose of affirmative action is the achievement of statistical parity (i.e., the race-sex composition of a company's labor force should approximate the underlying labor force base).

Impact of Population Representation

We should expect to see, other things being equal, minority group members achieving their largest gains in regions where they represent a relatively large proportion of the qualified labor force. To test the implications of this, we make use of Table V-2, which presents the racial distribution by region as taken from the 1970 census. Population distribution by race is used as a proxy for labor force distribution by race. It is recognized that, because of different age distributions, educational levels, and labor force participation rates among different races and sexes, population data distort the actual composition of the labor force in our nine regions. The distortion, however, is not of sufficient magnitude to invalidate our results.

Based on the concept of statistical parity, the following hypotheses were constructed using the distribution presented in the Table V-2:

1. Substantial gains for blacks should be experienced in the South Atlantic, East South Central, and West and Central regions.
2. Substantial gains for other minorities should also occur in the Mountain, Pacific, and West South Central regions.
3. Because there is a strong concentration of Hispanics in the Mountain, Pacific, and West South Central regions (and minimal density elsewhere), the largest proportion of substantial gains in a hypothesized region should be experienced by this group.

To confirm these hypotheses, we computed the number of substantial gains for each minority group in each of the five key occupational categories chosen for analysis. The total number of

TABLE V-2

Percent Distribution of the Population
by Region and Race, 1970

Region	Whites	Blacks	Hispanics	Other Minorities
New England	96.2	3.2	0.2	0.4
Middle Atlantic	88.5	10.6	0.3	0.6
South Atlantic	78.6	20.8	0.1	0.5
East North Central	89.8	9.6	0.2	0.4
East South Central	79.7	20.1	0.1	0.1
West North Central	94.9	4.3	0.1	0.7
West South Central	83.4	15.6	0.3	0.7
Mountain	94.2	2.2	0.4	3.2
Pacific	88.9	5.7	1.2	4.2

Source: U.S., Department of Commerce, Social and Economic Statistics Administration, Bureau of the Census, *General Population Characteristics, United States Summary*, Vol. PC (1)-B1 (Washington, D.C.: U.S. Government Printing Office, 1970), Table 60, p. 293.

Note: "Other Minorities" includes Orientals, other Asiatics, and Native American Indians.

substantial gains for each group was then subdivided into those that occurred in the hypothesized region and those that occurred in other regions. At least 66 percent of all substantial gains for minorities occurred where they are a relatively more numerous segment of the population than they are in other regions.

Table V-3 presents our results. Column 1 lists the total number of regions where minority group members achieved percentage gains in excess of their national average. Column 2 shows the number of these substantial gains for each minority group that occurred in the hypothesized region. Thus, for example, we see that black males, nationwide, achieved substantial gains in fifteen regions. Ten of these gains (66.7 percent) occurred in the South Atlantic, East South Central, and West South Central regions.

Thus, almost 70 percent of all substantial black gains occurred in the South Atlantic, East South Central, and West South Central regions. As one southern official stated: "We have been very fortunate with our intake of black workers. We have developed good relations with the predominantly black colleges and are able to attract the upper 10 percent of each year's graduating class."

This situation was directly reversed in the Midwest, where officials noted the paucity of technically trained blacks. Their complaint was echoed in all the interviews the authors conducted with operating companies located outside of the South.

TABLE V-3
*AT&T, Regional Distribution of Substantial Gains
by Race and Sex*

Race–Sex Group	Total Substantial Gains	Substantial Gains Occurring in Hypothesized Region	Percentage Occurring in Hypothesized Region
Black Males	15	10	66.7
Black Females	20	15	75.0
Hispanic Males	13	10	76.9
Hispanic Females	13	12	92.3
Other Males	10	8	80.0
Other Females	7	6	85.7

Source: The Company.

Hispanics and Other Minorities

As hypothesized, significant Hispanic advances were even more localized than those of the blacks, with 85 percent occurring in the three regions of highest population concentration. For purposes of analysis, Hispanics should be broken down into two groups: the Chicanos, or Mexican-Americans; and the Spanish-speaking immigrants from Latin America, Puerto Rico, and Cuba.

The primary group, the Chicanos, located largely in the Southwest and West, has experienced the greatest gains. Certain Cuban immigrants, especially the highly educated members of the middle class, who immigrated to the United States at the time of the Castro takeover, have also made advances, but they constitute only a small percentage of the available labor force and are concentrated in the Southeast, largely in Florida.

The remaining group, from Latin America and Puerto Rico, has failed to make a significant inroad in the AT&T labor force. Several reasons are given for this. Among those advanced, language problems and the lack of adequate training were most often noted in our interviews. As one midwestern official noted: "There will be an increasing need for technically trained people at our company. Hispanics have a very poor background in these areas and will be severely disadvantaged in terms of future employment prospects." Also, several officials throughout the country commented on the "language problem" as being a barrier to Hispanic advancement. In chapter IV, we noted that insistence on maintaining their language for everyday life added to communications problems for Hispanics.

With regard to the remaining protected group in our table, we see that substantial gains were also concentrated in the Southwest and

West. Other minority males and females achieved a combined total of 82.4 percent of their substantive advances in the Pacific and West South Central regions. These gains went largely to Oriental Americans. American Indians did very poorly because of apparent differences in cultural values and a reluctance to adapt to an urban environment.

Several officials surveyed commented on the "cultural problems" of Hispanics and Indians. One vice-president stated: "I would like to know the aspirations of these groups. Why are Hispanics and Indians so reluctant to accept our cultural values?" This reluctance was seen as working against the advancement of both Hispanics and Indians.

Locational Problems

Our interviews cast some doubts on the long-run viability of increasing minority representation. Several companies, widely dispersed throughout the country, noted that their growth areas were not in locations with high concentrations of minority group members. As one official stated:

> The growth in the demand for telephone services has occurred in areas with low populations of minority group members. We will not shift minority group workers to these regions for two reasons: Since the targets for these individuals will be lower in these areas due to their minimal population concentration, our company would not be working in its best interests to rotate protected group members there. Our aim is to fill local needs with local personnel. Secondly, our labor force is not highly mobile and would resist the transfer to another area.

This was echoed by another official who stated, "Minority group workers are reluctant to accept employment in the white suburbs, our high growth area." This lack of mobility and high concentration of minority group individuals in areas of declining opportunity for operating companies presages poorly for the future of affirmative action at AT&T.

Family Employment

One other interesting observation is in order. In the Midwest, operating companies had a tradition of "family employment" as two and three generations in a household took pride that they worked for the local telephone company. This, too, has been subverted to the needs of affirmative action, giving rise to morale problems. As one official noted: "There has been a tradition of family employment at our company. Fathers, acting as supervisors, would hire their sons. The fact that affirmative action no longer permits this has been a source of continual dissatisfaction among older employees."

DETAILED ANALYSIS OF
SELECTED OCCUPATIONAL GROUPS

Using the concept of covariance, we now proceed to a more extended analysis of the tradeoffs between race-sex groups in each of the five key job categories: officials and managers, sales workers, outside crafts, inside crafts, and clerical.

Our previous analysis has demonstrated that in each of these categories one race-sex group has experienced significant declines in percentage representation. In four of the five categories, white males bore this burden. Only in the clerical ranks did this trend reverse itself where white females were the sole group to experience declines in representation. In this section, we consider the remaining race-sex groups in each of our five occupational classifications and examine the tradeoffs between them. Our results provide insight into the competition among various protected groups for employment and promotion at AT&T.

Officials and Managers

Substantial gains for minority group members were regionally distributed according to population concentration. Black males and females achieved their strongest gains in the three southern regions; Hispanics and other minorities made their most significant gains in the Pacific, Mountain, and West South Central regions. All other areas showed gains for these groups that were below their nationwide average.

Several insights can be gained from an examination of Table V-4, which lists the negative covariances (tradeoffs) between race-sex groups (excluding white males) in the managerial ranks.

The first point worthy of note is that black males and females compete against all other protected groups for managerial employment. Black gains in percentage representation exhibit a negative covariance (tradeoff) with all other protected group members. The only other degree of competition that was found occurred between white females and Hispanic males. No other signs of competition among other race-sex groups were noted in the managerial ranks.

Second, blacks received their strongest competition from white females. The negative covariances between white females and black

TABLE V-4
AT&T, Tradeoff Analysis, Officials and Managers

	White Females	Hispanic Males	Other Minority Males	Hispanic Females	Other Minority Females
Black Males	-1.1983	-0.1171	-0.0853	-0.2419	-0.0822
Black Females	-1.4546	-0.1233	-0.0815	-0.2207	-0.0660
White Females	—	-0.4187	—	—	—

Source: Derived from Appendix V-A tables.

males (-1.1983) and between white females and black females (-1.4546) were the largest in an absolute value sense that were observed in the data for this occupational group. This should come as no surprise given our analysis from the preceding chapter in which we noted that white females were acting as a "block" to further black employment.

Tables V-5 and V-6 develop this point more forcefully. Nationwide, black male representation in management increased by 1.4 percent while that of black females also increased by 1.4 percent. The nationwide figure for white females was 2.4 percent. In the case of black males and white females, seven of the nine regions saw gains equal to or in excess of the national average for one group accompanied by gains below the nationwide figure for the second group. With black females and white females, the relationship was exactly the same. Seven of the nine regions showed gains above the national figure for one group accompanied by below-average gains for the second group. Such figures are evidence of a clear tradeoff between blacks (both male and female) and white females in management. Gains are defined as the change in percentage representation within management during the period 1973-79.

As can be seen from the tables, regions in which race-sex groups either exceeded or fell below their nationwide gain occurred twice in the case of both white females and black males (East North Central and East South Central regions) and in the case of white and black females (East South Central and Middle Atlantic regions).

A corollary of the above is that black males and females can be considered complements to each other. In three regions (South Atlantic, East South Central, and West South Central), both groups achieved gains in excess of their nationwide level. In four regions (New England, West North Central, Mountain, and Pacific), the gains of both black males and females were below the nationwide total. Only in the East North Central and Middle Atlantic regions were gains in excess of the nationwide level by one group (black

TABLE V-5

*AT&T, Comparison of Regional Gains in Management
Black Males and White Females*

Region	Black Males	White Females
New England	0.6	5.1
Middle Atlantic	1.2	2.9
South Atlantic	2.0	−1.0
East North Central[a]	1.2	2.2
West North Central	0.3	4.8
East South Central[a]	3.9	3.6
West South Central	2.1	−0.9
Mountain	0.3	5.5
Pacific	0.9	2.4

Source: Derived from Appendix V-A tables.

[a]Regions in which both race–sex groups exceeded or fell below their nationwide gain.

TABLE V-6

*AT&T, Comparison of Regional Gains in Management
Black Females and White Females*

Region	Black Females	White Females
New England	0.4	5.1
Middle Atlantic	1.5	2.9
South Atlantic	2.5	−1.0
East North Central	1.5	2.2
West North Central	0.4	4.8
East South Central[a]	3.5	3.6
West South Central	2.0	−0.9
Mountain	0.4	5.5
Pacific	1.2	2.4

Source: Derived from Appendix V-A tables.

[a]Regions in which both race–sex groups exceeded or fell below their nationwide gain.

females) accompanied by below nationwide level gains on the part of the other group (black males).

We noted above that blacks also compete against Hispanics and other minorities, but the degree of competition is negligible when compared with that posed by white females. As can be seen from Table V-3, the covariances between other minority groups and blacks are several orders of magnitude less than those between blacks and white females.

Several officials surveyed commented on this point. Although blacks operate at a comparative disadvantage vis-à-vis white females, the situation appears to be reversed with regard to members of other protected groups. One vice-president stated, "Although technically qualified blacks are not in vast supply, their numbers far outweigh those of other protected groups." Or, as another official noted: "We use assessment centers for promotion to management. Blacks do not perform well in these centers; however, Hispanics do even worse."

One remaining tradeoff to be noted from Table V-4 occurred between white females and Hispanic males. This was most noticeable in the West South Central region where white female representation declined by 0.9 percent while that of Hispanics rose by 2.2 percent.

In summary, then, at the managerial level, blacks, both male and female, compete against all other race-sex groups. They receive an especially strong challenge from white females. Their position relative to other protected group members is much stronger, a fact noted in many of our interviews.

Sales Workers

As with the previous occupational classification, significant gains for minority group members were distributed according to relative population density. Black gains were most noticeable in the South, although black females made substantial inroads in the East North Central region. Significant progress in representation by Hispanics and other protected group members occurred largely in the West and Southwest.

The tradeoffs were centered in the other male minority and Hispanic categories. As Table V-7 shows, other minority males traded off against blacks, white females, and other minority females, with white females providing the strongest competition. Also, Hispanic males again traded off very strongly against white females.

The inverse relationship between blacks and other males was most pronounced on the West Coast. In this region, blacks realized below-average gains in representation, while other minority males increased their share in excess of their nationwide total.

Outside Crafts

Although no tradeoffs among race-sex groups were noted in this category, other interesting points were observed. Primary among these was the reluctance of certain female groups to partake of outside craft employment.

TABLE V-7
AT&T, Tradeoff Analysis, Sales Workers

	Black Males	Black Females	White Females	Other Minority Females
Hispanic Males	—	−0.1765	−3.0085	−0.0893
Other Minority Males	−0.3750	−0.4960	−0.7003	−0.0719
Hispanic Females	−0.9537	−0.3345	—	0.5448

Source: Derived from Appendix V-A tables.

Specifically, our interviews noted an aversion to this form of employment among female graduates from Catholic schools, especially Irish Catholics. As one eastern official stated, "We have found a noticeable reluctance of the Irish Catholic females in our region to apply for nontraditional employment." A midwestern vice president echoed this, "We have seen that female graduates from parochial schools are less willing to seek employment in the nontraditional areas."

One other heavily Catholic group that also demonstrated a hesitancy in applying for outside craft work was found in the Cuban immigrant population in the Southeast. One official commented:

> The Hispanics here are quite well qualified since many of them came from an elite group in Cuba. This group has made great advances. Hispanic women, however, are often very reluctant to take jobs outside of the ordinary jobs for women. There is no 'if' problem about the willingness of women to move into nontraditional jobs, except for the Cuban women.

Thus, the drive for labor force parity can also reduce job opportunities even for members of protected groups. In order to achieve targets, nonmanagement opportunities for females have been drastically reduced in the operator and secretarial categories, the traditional areas of nonmanagerial female employment in the Bell System. Although all Bell operating companies have tremendously expanded the opportunities for females in outside and inside craft work, this is small compensation for women whose education and cultural background are not commensurate with this form of employment and who desire jobs as secretaries or operators.

Several other points require comment. As we pointed out in chapter III, accident rates in outside crafts decreased nationwide during the period of the consent decree. This reflects the increased emphasis on training and improved safety procedures throughout the Bell System. The reduction in accidents, however, was not distributed evenly along geographic lines or, as we saw in chapter III, along sex lines.

Table V-8 demonstrates that significant reductions in the female accident rate occurred in six of the nine regions. Only in the West and Southwest did this trend reverse itself resulting in a marked rise in the accident rate among females. Male injuries declined in eight of the nine regions, with only the mountain states showing a slight rise.

What accounts for the marked increase in female accident rates in the last three regions? All other areas showed declines in accidents among female workers. Why was this pattern reversed in the Southwest and West?

It is doubtful that geography and climate are significant factors. Although much of the area could be considered rough terrain, the authors discount this as a significant cause of increasing accidents among females for two reasons. First, as noted in chapter III, some companies, but not all, acknowledge that they follow a policy of not assigning females to regions which could be classified as harsh or inclement. Second, the female work force in these regions is concentrated in the more heavily developed urban areas where working conditions in outside crafts are relatively satisfactory. As one western official noted, "Women in outside crafts tend to be located near major cities since this is where the majority of the female employees in our company live."

The most satisfactory explanation for the rise in accident rates among females in these regions lies in the large number of females who have gained outside craft employment there since 1973. Table V-9 presents data on *average yearly* (not year-end) employment of females in outside crafts for 1973 and 1977. For convenience we divide the country into two groups: the six regions where female accident rates declined, forming Group I; and the remaining three regions constituting Group II.

Thus, female outside craft employment rose in the West and Southwest by an amount which exceeded the rise experienced by females in the remainder of the country. Over 53.4 percent of all new female employment in introductory craft positions came from the three regions of Group II.

The obvious consequence of such a surge in employment is a reduction in selectivity. The increase in accident rates among females is the logical result of a lowering of standards in an attempt to fill quotas for women in outside crafts. Such figures again cast serious doubt not only on the wisdom of statistical parity by sex in outside craft positions but also on the human decency of forcing it.

This fact is further supported by the data on retreat rates. One company official in Group II commented: "Our retreat rate is

TABLE V-8

AT&T, Geographical Distribution of Accidents per 100 Workers by Sex, Introductory Outside Crafts, 1973–77

| | 1973 | | 1977 | |
Region	Male	Female	Male	Female
New England	9.8	14.7	9.0	0.0
Middle Atlantic	14.7	38.7	10.8	22.0
South Atlantic	9.4	35.2	8.1	19.6
East North Central	20.1	58.0	13.1	32.1
West North Central	8.5	7.9	6.7	7.3
East South Central	7.3	76.7	7.1	32.1
West South Central	9.8	15.8	8.8	27.2
Mountain	7.1	6.1	7.3	24.0
Pacific	13.0	23.1	11.7	32.4

Source: The Company.

TABLE V-9

AT&T, Geographical Distribution of Average Female Employment Introductory Outside Crafts

	1973	1977	1977–1973
Group I	367	900	533
Group II	261	873	612
Percentage of Employment Accounted for by Group II	41.6	49.2	

Source: The Company.

fantastic. We have gone from 92 to 337 females in five years, but we have had to put 1,300 women on the job in order to retain the 337. Our male loss rate in these same jobs is only 9 percent." Such high turnover figures imply that the experience levels of the females in outside crafts are minimal at best. This lack of on-the-job experience is a prime cause of the rise in the accident rate among Group II companies. The situation should improve now that the company has reduced its goals for female outside craft workers from 19 to 9 percent.

Inside Crafts

Regionwide unanimity of opinion exists on the question of the ability of females to perform well in inside craft work. Operating companies have experienced no shortage of qualified women to fill job openings. Operational performance in this job category has increased with the improved utilization of female talent.

The regional data show that black males compete very strongly against white females for job openings in inside craft work. A smaller degree of competition was also found between Hispanic males and white females. Table V-10 presents these points.

As we saw in management, black males face strong competition from white females for the available job openings in inside crafts. White females made their strongest gains in the Southwest and West. Black males did not do as well in these regions but compensated for that with strong advances in the South. The regional distribution of gains for other minority group members is in accordance with the dispersion given in Table V-2.

Clerical

Problems exist in finding males of any race for this nontraditional form of employment. This shortage of supply of qualified males was a nationwide occurrence and led companies to such programs as initiating typing training for interested male candidates.

We have already seen competition between white females and black males for positions in management and inside crafts, positions made available by a decline in white male employment. A new rivalry is observed in the clerical ranks as white males compete against black males and females for the openings resulting, this time, from a reduction in white female opportunities. The degree of competition between white males and black females was especially strong. Black females contended against Hispanic males and other minority and females for available openings.

Of particular interest is the extreme rivalry between white males and black females. The covariance between the two groups of 1.9644 was one of the highest (absolute value sense) observed in the data. As is indicated in Appendix V-A, only in the West South Central and East North Central regions were substantial gains for both race-sex groups experienced. In the remaining seven regions, substantial gains for one party were accompanied by gains below the national figure for the second group.

Black female gains were especially strong in the South as should be expected. Again, all other minority group gains were distributed in accordance with the population distributions set forth in Table V-2.

TABLE V-10
AT&T, Tradeoff Analysis, Inside Crafts

	White Females
Black Males	-0.9172
Hispanic Males	-0.3711

Source: Derived from Appendix V-A tables.

TABLE V-11
AT&T, Tradeoff Analysis, Clerical

	White Males	Hispanic Males	Other Minority Males	Other Minority Females
Black Males	-0.1799	-0.0164	—	-0.0218
Black Females	-1.9644	-0.3906	-0.0889	-0.4697

Source: Derived from Appendix V-A tables.

SUMMARY

Our analysis has shown that minority group members achieved their greatest gains in regions where they represent a relatively significant proportion of the population. This is to be expected given the operational target of achieving statistical parity.

Nationwide, however, we noted strong competition between blacks and white females in management. Black males also competed against white females for inside craft positions. Black females were especially strong rivals with white males for clerical positions. Other tradeoffs between race-sex groups were noted as well.

With one exception, only positive covariances within a given job category were noted between males and females of the same racial group. The implication of this is that male and female partners of the same race were considered complements. That is, for example, if black males did well in a given region, black females tended, on average, to do well also. This held for all racial group and occupational categories except for a slight tradeoff between other minority males and females in the sales worker category.

A third result was that there are differences among racial groups. Thus, for example, we noted that although there was a shortage of technically trained blacks, their numbers far exceeded the available supply of Hispanics and other minorities, particularly American Indians. Hispanics suffer the additional handicaps of language and cultural differences, thereby compounding the problem of assimilating them into the AT&T labor force.

Minority group members do not form a homogeneous entity. Each brings to the labor market a different educational, cultural, and linguistic background. Companies pursuing equal employment opportunity on a nationwide scale must therefore realize that programs geared to increasing minority group representation must be tailored to the individual needs of blacks, Hispanics, Oriental Americans, and American Indians. A macro approach that treats all these different groups as a monolithic structure will not work.

The data also emphasize the competition of white females with minorities for the available job openings. A policy which applies affirmative action and/or quotas to females is by definition placing additional obstacles in the path of minority progress, especially where the background and education of the females may be superior to those of the minorities.

Finally, we examined regional differences in accident rates. We attributed the surge in accidents among females noted in the Southwest and West to the accelerated placement of women in outside craft positions in these regions. The high turnover among females resulted in a relatively inexperienced work force more easily susceptible to accidents. This again cast grave doubt on a governmental policy that, in effect, encourages such accidents in spite of elaborate company precautions and undoubtedly heavy expense to improve safety practices and conditions.

Appendix V-A

STATISTICAL TABLES

TABLE V-A-1

AT&T, Male Employment by Race and Occupational Group
New England Region, 1973 and 1979

Occupational Group	Male	Percent Male	1973 Black	Percent Black	Other Minorities	Percent Other Minorities
Officials and Managers	9,914	76.0	91	0.9	23	0.2
Administrative	173	9.1	10	5.8	3	1.7
Sales Workers	269	67.6	10	3.7	1	0.4
Clerical	878	5.7	48	5.5	12	1.4
Operators	322	3.3	12	3.7	2	0.6
Total White Collar	11,556	28.5	171	1.5	41	0.4
Outside Crafts	9,378	99.4	232	2.5	46	0.5
Inside Crafts	8,978	95.1	264	2.9	43	0.5
Service Workers	1,865	77.5	110	5.9	53	2.8
Total Blue Collar	20,221	95.0	606	3.0	142	0.7
Total	31,777	51.4	777	2.4	183	0.6

	1979					
	Male	Percent Male	Black	Percent Black	Other Minorities	Percent Other Minorities
Officials and Managers	9,950	70.3	179	1.8	47	0.5
Administrative	161	10.8	6	3.7	0	0.0
Sales Workers	241	55.0	11	4.6	1	0.4
Clerical	1,507	11.0	79	5.2	23	1.5
Operators	254	4.4	21	8.3	6	2.4
Total White Collar	12,113	34.0	296	2.4	77	0.6
Outside Crafts	7,630	99.2	138	1.8	32	0.4
Inside Crafts	6,168	92.1	147	2.4	23	0.4
Service Workers	1,255	80.7	62	4.9	24	1.9
Total Blue Collar	15,103	94.4	347	2.3	79	0.5
Total	27,216	52.7	643	2.4	156	0.6

TABLE V-A-2

AT&T, Female Employment by Race and Occupational Group
New England Region, 1973 and 1979

Occupational Group	Female	Percent Female	1973 Black	Percent Black	Other Minorities	Percent Other Minorities
Officials and Managers	3,135	24.0	87	2.8	11	0.4
Administrative	1,729	90.9	59	3.4	15	0.9
Sales Workers	129	32.4	14	10.9	1	0.8
Clerical	14,555	94.3	941	6.5	139	1.0
Operators	9,479	96.7	672	7.1	61	0.6
Total White Collar	29,027	71.5	1,773	6.1	227	0.8
Outside Crafts	58	0.6	0	0.0	1	1.7
Inside Crafts	466	4.9	22	4.7	2	0.4
Service Workers	540	22.5	20	3.7	3	0.6
Total Blue Collar	1,064	5.0	42	3.9	6	0.6
Total	30,091	48.6	1,815	6.0	233	0.8

	Female	Percent Female	Black	Percent Black	Other Minorities	Percent Other Minorities
			1979			
Officials and Managers	4,211	29.7	163	3.9	28	0.7
Administrative	1,333	89.2	69	5.2	9	0.7
Sales Workers	189	44.0	21	11.1	1	0.5
Clerical	12,193	89.0	998	8.2	94	0.8
Operators	5,572	95.6	339	6.1	27	0.5
Total White Collar	23,498	66.0	1,590	6.8	159	0.7
Outside Crafts	60	0.8	2	3.3	0	0.0
Inside Crafts	531	7.9	30	5.6	2	0.4
Service Workers	300	19.3	18	3.0	0	0.0
Total Blue Collar	891	5.6	50	5.6	2	0.2
Total	24,389	47.3	1,640	6.7	161	0.7

TABLE V-A-3

AT&T, Employment by Race and Occupational Group
New England Region, 1973 and 1979

Occupational Group	Total	1973 Black	Percent Black	Other Minorities	Percent Other Minorities
Officials and Managers	13,049	178	1.4	34	0.3
Administrative	1,902	69	3.6	18	0.9
Sales Workers	398	24	6.0	2	0.5
Clerical	15,433	989	6.4	151	1.0
Operators	9,801	684	7.0	63	0.6
Total White Collar	40,583	1,944	4.8	268	0.7
Outside Crafts	9,436	232	2.5	47	0.5
Inside Crafts	9,444	286	3.0	45	0.5
Service Workers	2,405	130	5.4	56	2.3
Total Blue Collar	21,285	648	3.0	148	0.7
Total	61,868	2,592	4.2	416	0.7

	Total	Black	1979 Percent Black	Other Minorities	Percent Other Minorities
Officials and Managers	14,161	342	2.4	75	0.5
Administrative	1,494	75	5.0	9	0.6
Sales Workers	430	32	7.4	2	0.5
Clerical	13,700	1,077	7.9	117	0.9
Operators	5,826	360	6.2	33	0.6
Total White Collar	35,611	1,886	5.3	236	0.7
Outside Crafts	7,740	140	1.8	32	0.4
Inside Crafts	6,699	177	2.6	25	0.4
Service Workers	1,555	80	5.1	24	1.5
Total Blue Collar	15,994	397	2.5	81	0.5
Total	51,605	2,283	4.4	317	0.6

TABLE V-A-4

AT&T, Employment by Sex and Occupational Group
New England Region, 1973 and 1979

Occupational Group	Total	1973 Male	Percent Male	Female	Percent Female
Officials and Managers	13,049	9,914	76.0	3,135	24.0
Administrative	1,902	173	9.1	1,729	90.9
Sales Workers	398	269	67.6	129	32.4
Clerical	15,433	878	5.7	14,555	94.3
Operators	9,801	322	3.3	9,479	96.7
Total White Collar	40,583	11,556	28.5	29,027	71.5
Outside Crafts	9,436	9,378	99.4	58	0.6
Inside Crafts	9,444	8,978	95.1	466	4.9
Service Workers	2,405	1,865	77.5	540	22.5
Total Blue Collar	21,285	20,221	95.0	1,064	5.0
Total	61,868	31,777	51.4	30,091	48.6

	Total	Male	Percent Male	Female	Percent Female
			1979		
Officials and Managers	14,161	9,950	70.3	4,211	29.7
Administrative	1,494	161	10.8	1,333	89.2
Sales Workers	430	241	56.0	189	44.0
Clerical	13,700	1,507	11.0	12,193	89.0
Operators	5,826	254	4.4	5,572	95.6
Total White Collar	35,611	12,113	34.0	23,498	66.0
Outside Crafts	7,740	7,680	99.2	60	0.8
Inside Crafts	6,699	6,168	92.1	531	7.9
Service Workers	1,555	1,255	80.7	300	19.3
Total Blue Collar	15,994	15,103	94.4	891	5.6
Total	51,605	27,216	52.7	24,389	47.3

TABLE V-A-5

AT&T, Percent Distribution by Race and Occupational Group
New England Region, 1973 and 1979

Occupational Group	1973			1979		
	All Employees	Blacks	Other Minorities	All Employees	Blacks	Other Minorities
Officials and Managers	21.1	6.9	8.1	27.4	15.0	23.7
Administrative	3.1	2.7	4.4	2.9	3.3	2.8
Sales Workers	0.6	0.9	0.5	0.8	1.4	0.6
Clerical	24.9	38.1	36.3	26.5	47.2	36.9
Operators	15.8	26.4	15.0	11.3	15.8	10.4
Total White Collar	65.5	75.0	64.3	68.9	82.7	74.4
Outside Crafts	15.3	9.0	11.3	15.0	6.1	10.1
Inside Crafts	15.3	11.0	10.6	13.0	7.8	7.9
Service Workers	3.9	5.0	13.8	3.1	3.4	7.6
Total Blue Collar	34.5	25.0	35.7	31.1	17.3	25.6
Total	100.0	100.0	100.0	100.0	100.0	100.0

TABLE V-A-6
AT&T, Percent Distribution by Sex and Occupational Group
New England Region, 1973 and 1979

Occupational Group	1973			1979		
	All Employees	Males	Females	All Employees	Males	Females
Officials and Managers	21.1	31.2	10.4	27.4	36.6	17.3
Administrative	3.1	0.5	5.7	2.9	0.6	5.5
Sales Workers	0.6	0.8	0.4	0.8	0.9	0.8
Clerical	24.9	2.8	48.4	26.5	5.5	50.0
Operators	15.8	1.0	31.5	11.3	0.9	22.8
Total White Collar	65.5	36.3	96.4	68.9	44.5	96.4
Outside Crafts	15.3	29.5	0.2	15.0	28.2	0.2
Inside Crafts	15.3	28.3	1.5	13.0	22.7	2.2
Service Workers	3.9	5.9	1.9	3.1	4.6	1.2
Total Blue Collar	34.5	63.7	3.6	31.1	55.5	3.6
Total	100.0	100.0	100.0	100.0	100.0	100.0

TABLE V-A-7

AT&T, Male Employment by Race and Occupational Group
Middle Atlantic Region, 1973 and 1979

Occupational Group	Male	Percent Male	Black	Percent Black	Other Minorities	Percent Other Minorities
				1973		
Officials and Managers	24,848	80.2	403	1.6	145	0.6
Administrative	755	8.5	79	10.5	25	3.3
Sales Workers	491	52.6	41	8.4	7	1.4
Clerical	2,639	6.7	602	22.8	228	8.6
Operators	778	3.3	128	16.4	19	2.4
Total White Collar	29,511	28.4	1,253	4.2	424	1.4
Outside Crafts	27,756	99.8	1,817	6.5	709	2.6
Inside Crafts	15,546	95.9	1,248	8.0	613	3.9
Service Workers	4,679	80.1	1,053	22.5	344	7.4
Total Blue Collar	47,981	96.2	4,118	8.6	1,666	3.5
Total	77,492	50.4	5,371	6.9	2,090	2.7

	Male	Percent Male	Black	Percent Black	Other Minorities	Percent Other Minorities
				1979		
Officials and Managers	24,549	75.5	808	3.3	328	1.3
Administrative	883	12.9	106	12.0	39	4.4
Sales Workers	662	61.2	79	11.4	34	4.9
Clerical	3,923	10.5	703	17.9	265	6.8
Operators	727	4.9	112	15.4	28	3.9
Total White Collar	30,774	33.1	1,808	5.9	694	2.3
Outside Crafts	24,220	98.8	1,568	6.5	696	2.9
Inside Crafts	14,979	90.5	1,308	8.7	618	4.1
Service Workers	1,345	64.6	394	29.3	148	11.0
Total Blue Collar	40,545	94.0	3,270	8.1	1,462	3.6
Total	71,319	52.4	5,078	7.1	2,156	3.0

TABLE V-A-8

*AT&T, Female Employment by Race and Occupational Group
Middle Atlantic Region, 1973 and 1979*

| | 1973 | | | | | |
Occupational Group	Female	Percent Female	Black	Percent Black	Other Minorities	Percent Other Minorities
Officials and Managers	6,140	19.8	437	7.1	62	1.0
Administrative	8,105	91.5	1,163	14.3	169	2.1
Sales Workers	442	47.4	73	16.5	14	3.2
Clerical	36,694	93.3	8,453	23.0	1,113	3.0
Operators	22,902	96.7	7,464	32.6	348	1.5
Total White Collar	74,283	71.6	17,590	23.7	1,706	2.3
Outside Crafts	68	0.2	5	7.5	1	1.5
Inside Crafts	668	4.1	120	18.0	15	2.2
Service Workers	1,161	19.9	239	20.6	20	1.7
Total Blue Collar	1,897	3.8	364	19.2	36	1.9
Total	76,180	49.6	17,954	23.6	1,742	2.3

	Female	Percent Female	Black	Percent Black	Other Minorities	Percent Other Minorities
			1979			
Officials and Managers	7,981	24.5	941	11.8	170	2.1
Administrative	5,959	87.1	1,221	20.5	213	3.6
Sales Workers	438	38.8	97	22.1	15	3.4
Clerical	33,555	89.5	9,536	28.4	1,178	3.5
Operators	14,237	95.1	4,739	33.3	275	1.9
Total White Collar	62,170	66.9	16,534	26.6	1,851	3.0
Outside Crafts	293	1.2	48	16.4	10	3.4
Inside Crafts	1,554	9.4	323	20.8	46	3.0
Service Workers	739	35.4	176	23.8	22	3.0
Total Blue Collar	2,586	6.0	547	21.2	78	3.0
Total	64,756	47.6	17,081	26.4	1,929	3.0

TABLE V-A-9

AT&T, Employment by Race and Occupational Group
Middle Atlantic Region, 1973 and 1979

Occupational Group	Total	Black	1973 Percent Black	Other Minorities	Percent Other Minorities
Officials and Managers	30,988	840	2.7	207	0.7
Administrative	8,860	1,242	14.0	194	2.2
Sales Workers	933	114	12.2	21	2.3
Clerical	39,333	9,055	23.0	1,341	3.4
Operators	23,680	7,592	32.1	367	1.5
Total White Collar	103,794	18,843	18.2	2,130	2.1
Outside Crafts	27,824	1,822	6.5	710	2.6
Inside Crafts	16,214	1,368	8.4	628	3.9
Service Workers	5,840	1,292	22.1	364	6.2
Total Blue Collar	49,878	4,482	9.0	1,702	3.4
Total	153,672	23,325	15.2	3,832	2.5

			1979		
	Total	Black	Percent Black	Other Minorities	Percent Other Minorities
Officials and Managers	32,530	1,749	5.4	498	1.5
Administrative	6,842	1,327	19.4	252	3.7
Sales Workers	1,130	176	15.6	49	4.3
Clerical	37,478	10,239	27.3	1,443	3.9
Operators	14,964	4,851	32.4	303	2.0
Total White Collar	92,944	18,342	19.7	2,545	2.7
Outside Crafts	24,513	1,616	6.6	706	2.9
Inside Crafts	16,533	1,631	9.9	664	4.0
Service Workers	2,085	570	27.3	170	8.2
Total Blue Collar	43,131	3,817	8.3	1,540	3.6
Total	136,075	22,159	16.3	4,085	3.0

TABLE V-A-10

*AT&T, Employment by Sex and Occupational Group
Middle Atlantic Region, 1973 and 1979*

Occupational Group	Total	Male	1973 Percent Male	Female	Percent Female
Officials and Managers	30,988	24,848	80.2	6,140	19.8
Administrative	8,860	755	8.5	8,105	91.5
Sales Workers	933	491	52.6	442	47.4
Clerical	39,333	2,639	6.7	36,694	93.3
Operators	23,680	778	3.3	22,902	96.7
Total White Collar	103,794	29,511	28.4	74,283	71.6
Outside Crafts	27,824	27,756	99.8	68	0.2
Inside Crafts	16,214	15,546	95.9	668	4.1
Service Workers	5,840	4,679	80.1	1,161	19.9
Total Blue Collar	49,878	47,981	96.2	1,897	3.8
Total	153,672	77,492	50.4	76,180	49.6

| | | 1979 | | |
	Total	Male	Percent Male	Female	Percent Female
Officials and Managers	32,550	24,549	75.5	7,981	24.5
Administrative	6,842	883	12.9	5,959	87.1
Sales Workers	1,150	692	61.2	438	38.8
Clerical	37,478	3,923	10.5	33,555	89.5
Operators	14,964	727	4.9	14,237	95.1
Total White Collar	92,944	30,774	33.1	62,170	66.9
Outside Crafts	24,513	24,220	98.8	293	1.2
Inside Crafts	16,533	14,979	90.6	1,554	9.4
Service Workers	2,085	1,346	64.6	739	35.4
Total Blue Collar	43,131	40,545	94.0	2,586	6.0
Total	136,075	71,319	52.4	64,756	47.6

TABLE V-A-11
AT&T, Percent Distribution by Race and Occupational Group
Middle Atlantic Region, 1973 and 1979

Occupational Group	1973			1979		
	All Employees	Blacks	Other Minorities	All Employees	Blacks	Other Minorities
Officials and Managers	20.2	3.4	5.1	23.9	7.9	12.2
Administrative	5.8	5.3	5.1	5.0	6.0	6.2
Sales Workers	0.6	0.5	0.6	0.8	0.8	1.2
Clerical	25.6	38.8	35.0	27.5	46.2	35.3
Operators	15.4	32.6	9.6	11.0	21.9	7.4
Total White Collar	67.6	80.6	55.4	68.2	82.8	62.3
Outside Crafts	18.1	7.8	18.5	18.0	7.3	17.3
Inside Crafts	10.6	5.9	16.4	12.1	7.4	16.3
Service Workers	3.7	5.7	9.7	1.7	2.5	4.1
Total Blue Collar	32.4	19.4	44.6	31.8	17.2	37.7
Total	100.0	100.0	100.0	100.0	100.0	100.0

TABLE V-A-12

AT&T, Percent Distribution by Sex and Occupational Group
Middle Atlantic Region, 1973 and 1979

Occupational Group	1973			1979		
	All Employees	Males	Females	All Employees	Males	Females
Officials and Managers	20.2	32.1	8.1	23.9	34.4	12.3
Administrative	5.8	1.0	10.6	5.0	1.2	9.2
Sales Workers	0.6	0.7	0.5	0.8	1.0	0.7
Clerical	25.6	3.4	48.2	27.5	5.5	51.8
Operators	15.4	1.0	30.1	11.0	1.0	22.0
Total White Collar	67.6	38.2	97.6	68.2	43.1	96.0
Outside Crafts	18.1	35.8	0.1	18.0	34.0	0.5
Inside Crafts	10.6	20.1	0.9	12.1	21.0	2.4
Service Workers	3.7	5.9	1.4	1.7	1.9	1.1
Total Blue Collar	32.4	61.8	2.4	31.8	56.9	4.0
Total	100.0	100.0	100.0	100.0	100.0	100.0

TABLE V-A-13
AT&T, Male Employment by Race and Occupational Group
South Atlantic Region, 1973 and 1979

Occupational Group	1973					
	Male	Percent Male	Black	Percent Black	Other Minorities	Percent Other Minorities
Officials and Managers	16,464	72.7	396	2.4	156	0.9
Administrative	85	3.2	20	23.5	0	0.0
Sales Workers	915	74.1	48	5.2	18	2.0
Clerical	1,109	3.8	196	17.7	38	3.4
Operators	926	3.9	191	20.6	26	2.8
Total White Collar	19,499	24.5	851	4.4	238	1.2
Outside Crafts	22,835	99.4	1,655	7.2	375	1.6
Inside Crafts	9,802	81.4	583	5.9	143	1.5
Service Workers	2,132	87.3	1,064	49.9	74	3.5
Total Blue Collar	34,769	92.8	3,302	9.5	592	1.7
Total	54,268	46.4	4,153	7.7	830	1.5

	Male	Percent Male	Black	Percent Black	Other Minorities	Percent Other Minorities
			1979			
Officials and Managers	18,039	71.1	965	5.3	242	1.3
Administrative	222	6.0	45	20.3	11	5.0
Sales Workers	1,126	59.0	133	11.8	35	3.1
Clerical	2,037	6.4	457	22.4	130	6.4
Operators	899	6.2	169	18.8	36	4.0
Total White Collar	22,323	28.8	1,769	7.9	465	2.1
Outside Crafts	21,961	95.5	1,760	8.0	410	1.9
Inside Crafts	10,261	75.8	1,071	10.4	185	1.8
Service Workers	424	62.9	311	73.3	21	5.0
Total Blue Collar	32,645	87.8	3,142	9.6	616	1.9
Total	54,969	47.9	4,911	8.9	1,081	2.0

TABLE V-A-14
*AT&T, Female Employment by Race and Occupational Group
South Atlantic Region, 1973 and 1979*

Occupational Group	1973					
	Female	Percent Female	Black	Percent Black	Other Minorities	Percent Other Minorities
Officials and Managers	6,176	27.3	417	6.8	59	1.0
Administrative	2,600	96.8	188	7.2	27	1.0
Sales Workers	320	25.9	33	10.3	8	2.5
Clerical	28,094	96.2	4,781	17.0	569	2.0
Operators	22,927	96.1	6,013	26.2	198	0.9
Total White Collar	60,117	75.5	11,432	19.0	861	1.4
Outside Crafts	149	0.6	9	6.1	0	0.0
Inside Crafts	2,241	18.6	222	9.9	13	0.6
Service Workers	310	12.7	196	63.2	7	2.3
Total Blue Collar	2,700	7.2	427	15.8	20	0.7
Total	62,817	53.6	11,859	18.9	881	1.4

			1979			
	Female	Percent Female	Black	Percent Black	Other Minorities	Percent Other Minorities
Officials and Managers	7,349	28.9	1,087	14.8	125	1.7
Administrative	3,466	94.0	484	14.0	94	2.7
Sales Workers	782	41.0	152	19.4	28	3.6
Clerical	29,975	93.6	6,730	22.5	803	2.7
Operators	13,689	93.8	3,585	26.2	319	2.3
Total White Collar	55,261	71.2	12,038	21.8	1,369	2.5
Outside Crafts	1,025	4.5	218	21.3	19	1.9
Inside Crafts	3,268	24.2	497	15.2	50	1.5
Service Workers	250	37.1	124	49.6	19	7.6
Total Blue Collar	4,543	12.2	839	18.5	88	1.9
Total	59,804	52.1	12,877	21.5	1,457	2.4

TABLE V-A-15

AT&T, Employment by Race and Occupational Group
South Atlantic Region, 1973 and 1979

Occupational Group	Total	1973			
		Black	Percent Black	Other Minorities	Percent Other Minorities
Officials and Managers	22,640	813	3.6	215	0.9
Administrative	2,685	208	7.7	27	1.0
Sales Workers	1,235	81	6.6	26	2.1
Clerical	29,203	4,977	17.0	607	2.1
Operators	23,853	6,204	26.0	224	0.9
Total White Collar	79,616	12,283	15.4	1,099	1.4
Outside Crafts	22,984	1,664	7.2	375	1.6
Inside Crafts	12,043	805	6.7	156	1.3
Service Workers	2,442	1,260	51.6	81	3.3
Total Blue Collar	37,469	3,729	10.0	612	1.6
Total	117,085	16,012	13.7	1,711	1.5

	Total	Black	Percent Black	Other Minorities	Percent Other Minorities
			1979		
Officials and Managers	25,388	2,052	8.1	367	1.4
Administrative	3,688	529	14.3	105	2.8
Sales Workers	1,908	285	14.9	63	3.3
Clerical	32,012	7,187	22.5	933	2.9
Operators	14,583	3,754	25.7	355	2.4
Total White Collar	77,584	13,807	17.3	1,823	2.3
Outside Crafts	22,986	1,978	8.6	429	1.9
Inside Crafts	13,529	1,568	11.6	235	1.7
Service Workers	674	435	64.5	40	5.9
Total Blue Collar	37,189	3,981	10.7	704	1.9
Total	114,773	17,788	15.5	2,527	2.2

TABLE V-A-16
AT&T, Employment by Sex and Occupational Group
South Atlantic Region, 1973 and 1979

Occupational Group			1973		
	Total	Male	Percent Male	Female	Percent Female
Officials and Managers	22,640	16,464	72.7	6,176	27.3
Administrative	2,685	85	3.2	2,600	96.8
Sales Workers	1,235	915	74.1	320	25.9
Clerical	29,203	1,109	3.8	28,094	96.2
Operators	23,853	926	3.9	22,927	96.1
Total White Collar	79,616	19,499	24.5	60,117	75.5
Outside Crafts	22,984	22,835	99.4	149	0.6
Inside Crafts	12,043	9,802	81.4	2,241	18.6
Service Workers	2,442	2,132	87.3	310	12.7
Total Blue Collar	37,469	34,769	92.8	2,700	7.2
Total	117,085	54,268	46.4	62,817	53.6

	Total	1979			
		Male	Percent Male	Female	Percent Female
Officials and Managers	25,388	18,039	71.1	7,349	28.9
Administrative	3,688	222	6.0	3,466	94.0
Sales Workers	1,908	1,126	59.0	782	41.0
Clerical	32,012	2,037	6.4	29,975	93.6
Operators	14,588	899	6.2	13,689	93.8
Total White Collar	77,584	22,323	28.8	55,261	71.2
Outside Crafts	22,986	21,961	95.5	1,025	4.5
Inside Crafts	13,529	10,261	75.8	3,268	24.2
Service Workers	674	424	62.9	250	37.1
Total Blue Collar	37,189	32,646	87.8	4,543	12.2
Total	114,773	54,969	47.9	59,804	52.1

TABLE V-A-17
AT&T, Percent Distribution by Race and Occupational Group
South Atlantic Region, 1973 and 1979

Occupational Group	1973			1979		
	All Employees	Blacks	Other Minorities	All Employees	Blacks	Other Minorities
Officials and Managers	19.3	5.1	12.5	22.1	11.5	14.5
Administrative	2.3	1.3	1.6	3.2	3.0	4.2
Sales Workers	1.1	0.5	1.6	1.7	1.6	2.5
Clerical	24.9	31.0	35.4	27.9	40.4	36.9
Operators	20.4	38.8	13.1	12.7	21.1	14.0
Total White Collar	68.0	76.7	64.2	67.6	77.6	72.1
Outside Crafts	19.6	10.4	21.8	20.0	11.1	17.0
Inside Crafts	10.3	5.0	9.1	11.8	8.8	9.3
Service Workers	2.1	7.9	4.9	0.6	2.5	1.6
Total Blue Collar	32.0	23.3	35.8	32.4	22.4	27.9
Total	100.0	100.0	100.0	100.0	100.0	100.0

TABLE V-A-15
AT&T, *Percent Distribution by Sex and Occupational Group
South Atlantic Region, 1973 and 1979*

Occupational Group	1973			1979		
	All Employees	Males	Females	All Employees	Males	Females
Officials and Managers	19.5	30.3	9.8	22.1	32.8	12.3
Administrative	2.3	0.2	4.2	3.2	0.4	5.8
Sales Workers	1.1	1.8	0.5	1.7	2.0	1.3
Clerical	24.9	2.0	44.5	27.9	3.7	50.1
Operators	20.4	1.7	36.5	12.7	1.6	22.9
Total White Collar	68.0	36.0	95.6	67.6	40.5	92.4
Outside Crafts	19.6	42.0	0.2	20.0	40.0	1.7
Inside Crafts	10.3	18.1	3.6	11.8	18.7	5.5
Service Workers	2.1	3.9	0.6	0.6	0.8	0.4
Total Blue Collar	32.0	64.0	4.4	32.4	59.5	7.6
Total	100.0	100.0	100.0	100.0	100.0	100.0

TABLE V-A-19

AT&T, Male Employment by Race and Occupational Group
East North Central Region, 1973 and 1979

Occupational Group	1973						
	Male	Percent Male	Black	Percent Black	Other Minorities	Percent Other Minorities
Officials and Managers	20,395	75.6	564	2.8	46	0.2
Administrative	314	7.1	22	7.1	5	1.6
Sales Workers	571	72.4	48	8.4	1	0.2
Clerical	2,088	6.4	245	12.1	70	3.4
Operators	806	3.9	188	23.2	27	3.3
Total White Collar	24,174	28.4	1,067	4.4	149	0.6
Outside Crafts	22,175	99.4	1,341	6.0	183	0.8
Inside Crafts	11,302	88.7	686	6.1	102	0.9
Service Workers	4,090	70.4	1,039	25.4	108	2.6
Total Blue Collar	37,567	91.9	3,066	8.2	393	1.0
Total	61,741	49.1	4,133	6.7	542	0.9

	Male	Percent Male	Black	Percent Black	Other Minorities	Percent Other Minorities
			1979			
Officials and Managers	20,118	71.8	930	4.6	129	0.6
Administrative	1,055	19.4	113	10.3	26	2.4
Sales Workers	55	59.4	67	12.1	13	2.3
Clerical	3,939	12.2	633	16.1	182	4.6
Operators	1,184	7.9	261	22.0	45	3.8
Total White Collar	26,891	32.8	2,004	7.5	395	1.5
Outside Crafts	19,633	97.1	1,123	5.7	205	1.0
Inside Crafts	11,590	83.4	857	7.4	133	1.1
Service Workers	1,415	47.9	472	33.3	57	4.0
Total Blue Collar	32,646	88.0	2,452	7.5	395	1.2
Total	59,537	50.0	4,456	7.5	790	1.3

TABLE V-A-20

AT&T, Female Employment by Race and Occupational Group
East North Central Region, 1973 and 1979

Occupational Group	1973					
	Female	Percent Female	Black	Percent Black	Other Minorities	Percent Other Minorities
Officials and Managers	6,570	24.4	682	10.4	40	0.6
Administrative	4,118	92.9	403	9.8	25	0.6
Sales Workers	218	27.6	27	12.4	3	1.4
Clerical	29,608	93.6	5,669	19.1	425	1.4
Operators	20,108	96.1	4,056	20.2	234	1.2
Total White Collar	60,622	71.6	10,837	17.8	727	1.2
Outside Crafts	138	0.6	16	11.8	0	0.0
Inside Crafts	1,445	11.3	271	2.1	19	0.1
Service Workers	1,717	29.6	648	44.8	21	1.5
Total Blue Collar	3,300	8.1	935	28.3	40	1.2
Total	63,922	50.9	11,772	18.4	767	1.2

	Female	Percent Female	Black	Percent Black	Other Minorities	Percent Other Minorities
				1979		
Officials and Managers	7,921	28.2	1,133	14.3	98	1.2
Administrative	4,562	80.6	780	17.1	102	2.2
Sales Workers	379	40.6	70	18.5	8	2.1
Clerical	28,461	87.8	6,908	24.3	710	2.5
Operators	13,746	92.1	2,778	20.2	310	2.3
Total White Collar	55,069	67.8	11,669	21.2	1,228	2.2
Outside Crafts	582	2.9	87	14.9	12	2.1
Inside Crafts	2,310	16.6	450	19.5	38	1.6
Service Workers	1,541	52.1	542	35.2	34	2.2
Total Blue Collar	4,433	12.0	1,079	24.3	84	1.9
Total	59,502	50.0	12,748	21.4	1,312	2.2

TABLE V-A-21

AT&T, Employment by Race and Occupational Group

East North Central Region, 1973 and 1979

Occupational Group	Total	Black	1973 Percent Black	Other Minorities	Percent Other Minorities
Officials and Managers	26,965	1,246	4.6	86	0.3
Administrative	4,432	425	9.6	30	0.7
Sales Workers	789	75	9.5	4	0.5
Clerical	31,696	5,914	18.6	495	1.6
Operators	20,914	4,244	20.3	261	1.2
Total White Collar	84,796	11,904	14.0	876	1.0
Outside Crafts	22,313	1,357	6.1	183	0.8
Inside Crafts	12,747	957	7.5	121	0.9
Service Workers	5,807	1,687	29.1	129	2.2
Total Blue Collar	40,867	4,001	9.8	433	1.1
Total	125,663	15,905	12.7	1,309	1.0

	Total	1979 Black	Percent Black	Other Minorities	Percent Other Minorities
Officials and Managers	28,039	2,063	7.4	227	0.8
Administrative	5,657	893	15.8	128	2.3
Sales Workers	934	137	14.7	21	2.2
Clerical	32,400	7,541	23.3	892	2.8
Operators	14,930	3,039	20.4	355	2.4
Total White Collar	81,960	13,673	16.7	1,623	2.0
Outside Crafts	20,220	1,210	6.0	217	1.1
Inside Crafts	13,900	1,307	9.4	171	1.2
Service Workers	2,959	1,014	34.3	91	3.1
Total Blue Collar	37,079	3,531	9.5	479	1.3
Total	119,039	17,204	14.5	2,102	1.8

TABLE V-A-22

AT&T, Employment by Sex and Occupational Group
East North Central Region, 1973 and 1979

Occupational Group	Total	1973				
		Male	Percent Male	Female	Percent Female	
Officials and Managers	26,695	20,395	75.6	6,570	24.4	
Administrative	4,432	314	7.1	4,118	92.9	
Sales Workers	789	571	72.4	218	27.6	
Clerical	31,696	2,088	6.4	29,608	93.6	
Operators	20,914	806	3.9	20,108	96.1	
Total White Collar	84,796	24,174	28.8	60,622	71.6	
Outside Crafts	22,313	22,175	99.4	138	0.6	
Inside Crafts	12,747	11,302	88.7	1,445	11.3	
Service Workers	5,807	4,090	70.4	1,717	29.6	
Total Blue Collar	40,867	37,567	91.9	3,300	8.1	
Total	125,663	61,741	49.1	63,992	50.9	

	Total	Male	Percent Male	Female	Percent Female
			1979		
Officials and Managers	28,039	20,118	71.8	7,291	28.2
Administrative	5,657	1,095	19.4	4,562	80.6
Sales Workers	934	555	59.4	379	40.6
Clerical	32,400	3,939	12.2	28,461	87.8
Operators	14,930	1,184	7.9	13,746	92.1
Total White Collar	81,960	26,891	32.8	55,069	67.8
Outside Crafts	20,220	19,638	97.1	582	2.9
Inside Crafts	13,900	11,590	83.4	2,310	16.6
Service Workers	2,959	1,418	47.9	1,541	52.1
Total Blue Collar	37,079	32,646	88.0	4,433	12.0
Total	119,039	59,537	50.0	59,502	50.0

TABLE V-A-23

AT&T, Percent Distribution by Race and Occupational Group
East North Central Region, 1973 and 1979

Occupational Group	1973			1979		
	All Employees	Blacks	Other Minorities	All Employees	Blacks	Other Minorities
Officials and Managers	21.5	7.9	6.6	23.6	12.0	10.8
Administrative	3.5	2.7	2.3	4.8	5.2	6.1
Sales Workers	0.6	0.5	0.3	0.8	0.8	1.0
Clerical	25.3	37.2	37.8	27.2	43.8	42.4
Operators	16.6	26.6	19.9	12.5	17.7	16.9
Total White Collar	67.5	74.9	66.9	68.9	79.5	77.2
Outside Crafts	17.7	8.5	13.9	17.0	7.0	10.3
Inside Crafts	10.1	6.0	9.2	11.7	7.6	8.1
Service Workers	4.7	10.6	10.0	2.4	5.9	4.4
Total Blue Collar	32.5	25.1	33.1	31.1	20.5	22.8
Total	100.0	100.0	100.0	100.0	100.0	100.0

TABLE V-A-24

AT&T, Percent Distribution by Sex and Occupational Group
East North Central Region, 1973 and 1979

Occupational Group	1973			1979		
	All Employees	Males	Females	All Employees	Males	Females
Officials and Managers	21.5	33.1	10.3	23.6	33.8	13.3
Administrative	3.5	0.5	6.5	4.8	1.8	7.7
Sales Workers	0.6	0.9	0.3	0.8	0.9	0.6
Clerical	25.3	3.3	46.5	27.2	6.6	47.8
Operators	16.6	1.3	31.3	12.5	2.0	23.1
Total White Collar	67.5	39.1	94.8	68.9	45.1	92.5
Outside Crafts	17.7	35.9	0.2	17.0	33.0	1.0
Inside Crafts	10.1	18.3	2.3	11.7	19.5	3.9
Service Workers	4.7	6.7	2.7	2.4	2.4	2.6
Total Blue Collar	32.5	60.9	5.2	31.1	54.9	7.5
Total	100.0	100.0	100.0	100.0	100.0	100.0

TABLE V-A-25

AT&T, Male Employment by Race and Occupational Group
East South Central Region, 1973 and 1979

| Occupational Group | Male | Percent Male | 1973 | | | |
			Black	Percent Black	Other Minorities	Percent Other Minorities
Officials and Managers	6,517	79.8	67	1.0	4	0.1
Administrative	591	21.4	61	10.3	8	1.4
Sales Workers	304	75.8	9	3.0	1	0.3
Clerical	369	2.8	81	22.0	0	0.0
Operators	488	3.8	92	18.9	1	0.2
Total White Collar	8,269	22.3	310	3.7	14	0.2
Outside Crafts	11,437	99.6	1,323	11.6	14	0.1
Inside Crafts	4,418	82.4	208	4.7	4	0.1
Service Workers	718	81.5	442	61.6	1	0.1
Total Blue Collar	16,573	93.5	1,973	11.9	19	0.1
Total	24,842	45.3	2,283	9.2	33	0.1

		1979				
	Male	Percent Male	Black	Percent Black	Other Minorities	Percent Other Minorities
Officials and Managers	9,140	72.6	600	6.6	42	0.5
Administrative	147	6.0	25	17.0	0	0.0
Sales Workers	337	58.6	51	15.1	4	1.2
Clerical	1,284	7.6	295	23.0	8	0.6
Operators	549	5.6	135	24.6	0	0.0
Total White Collar	11,457	27.1	1,106	9.7	54	0.5
Outside Crafts	11,170	94.4	1,142	10.2	39	0.3
Inside Crafts	4,067	76.2	313	7.7	13	0.3
Service Workers	687	70.8	332	48.3	1	0.1
Total Blue Collar	15,924	87.8	1,787	11.2	53	0.3
Total	27,381	45.4	2,893	10.6	107	0.4

TABLE V-A-26

AT&T, Female Employment by Race and Occupational Group
East South Central Region, 1973 and 1979

Occupational Group	Female	Percent Female	Black	1973 Percent Black	Other Minorities	Percent Other Minorities
Officials and Managers	1,653	20.2	25	1.5	0	0.0
Administrative	2,173	78.6	79	3.6	7	0.3
Sales Workers	97	24.2	4	4.1	0	0.0
Clerical	12,658	97.2	1,552	12.3	18	0.1
Operators	12,225	96.2	3,025	24.7	30	0.2
Total White Collar	28,806	77.7	4,685	16.3	55	0.2
Outside Crafts	46	0.4	3	6.5	0	0.0
Inside Crafts	944	17.6	53	5.6	1	0.1
Service Workers	163	18.5	123	75.5	0	0.0
Total Blue Collar	1,153	6.5	179	15.5	1	0.1
Total	29,959	54.7	4,864	16.2	56	0.2

	Female	Percent Female	Black	Percent Black	Other Minorities	Percent Other Minorities
				1979		
Officials and Managers	3,449	27.4	478	13.9	18	0.5
Administrative	2,302	94.0	326	14.2	7	0.3
Sales Workers	238	41.4	46	19.3	0	0.0
Clerical	15,573	92.4	3,217	20.7	76	0.5
Operators	9,195	94.4	2,625	28.5	46	0.5
Total White Collar	30,757	72.9	6,692	21.8	147	0.5
Outside Crafts	667	5.6	136	20.4	1	0.1
Inside Crafts	1,273	23.8	161	12.6	4	0.3
Service Workers	283	29.2	115	40.6	0	0.0
Total Blue Collar	2,223	12.2	412	18.5	5	0.2
Total	32,980	54.6	7,104	21.5	152	0.5

TABLE V-A-27

*AT&T, Employment by Race and Occupational Group
East South Central Region, 1973 and 1979*

Occupational Group	Total	1973 Black	Percent Black	Other Minorities	Percent Other Minorities
Officials and Managers	8,170	92	1.1	4	0.1
Administrative	2,764	140	5.1	15	0.5
Sales Workers	401	13	3.2	1	0.2
Clerical	13,027	1,633	12.5	18	0.1
Operators	12,713	3,117	24.5	31	0.2
Total White Collar	37,075	4,995	13.5	69	0.2
Outside Crafts	11,483	1,326	11.5	14	0.1
Inside Crafts	5,362	261	4.9	5	0.1
Service Workers	881	565	64.1	1	0.1
Total Blue Collar	17,726	2,152	12.1	20	0.1
Total	54,801	7,147	13.0	89	0.2

	Total	Black	1979 Percent Black	Other Minorities	Percent Other Minorities
Officials and Managers	12,589	1,078	8.5	60	0.5
Administrative	2,449	351	14.3	7	0.3
Sales Workers	575	97	16.9	4	0.7
Clerical	16,857	3,512	20.8	84	0.5
Operators	9,744	2,760	28.3	46	0.5
Total White Collar	42,214	7,798	18.5	201	0.5
Outside Crafts	11,837	1,278	10.8	40	0.3
Inside Crafts	5,340	474	8.9	17	0.3
Service Workers	970	447	46.1	1	0.1
Total Blue Collar	18,147	2,139	12.1	58	0.3
Total	60,361	9,997	16.6	259	0.4

TABLE V-A-28

AT&T, Employment by Sex and Occupational Group
East South Central Region, 1973 and 1979

Occupational Group	Total	Male	1973 Percent Male	Female	Percent Female
Officials and Managers	8,170	6,517	79.8	1,653	20.2
Administrative	2,764	591	21.4	2,173	78.6
Sales Workers	401	304	75.8	97	24.2
Clerical	13,027	369	2.8	12,658	97.2
Operators	12,713	488	3.8	12,225	96.2
Total White Collar	37,075	8,269	22.3	28,806	77.7
Outside Crafts	11,483	11,437	99.6	46	0.4
Inside Crafts	5,362	4,418	82.4	944	17.6
Service Workers	881	718	81.5	163	18.5
Total Blue Collar	17,726	16,573	93.5	1,153	6.5
Total	54,801	24,842	45.3	29,959	54.7

	Total	Male	1979 Percent Male	Female	Percent Female
Officials and Managers	12,589	9,140	72.6	3,449	27.4
Administrative	2,449	147	6.0	2,302	94.0
Sales Workers	575	337	58.6	238	41.4
Clerical	16,857	1,284	7.6	15,573	92.4
Operators	9,744	549	5.6	9,195	94.4
Total White Collar	42,214	11,457	27.1	30,757	72.9
Outside Crafts	11,837	11,170	94.4	667	5.6
Inside Crafts	5,340	4,067	76.2	1,273	23.8
Service Workers	970	687	70.8	283	29.2
Total Blue Collar	18,147	15,924	87.8	2,223	12.2
Total	60,361	27,381	45.4	32,980	54.6

TABLE V-A-29

AT&T, Percent Distribution by Race and Occupational Group
East South Central Region, 1973 and 1979

Occupational Group	1973			1979		
	All Employees	Blacks	Other Minorities	All Employees	Blacks	Other Minorities
Officials and Managers	14.9	1.3	4.5	20.9	10.8	23.2
Administrative	5.0	2.0	16.9	4.1	3.5	2.7
Sales Workers	0.7	0.2	1.1	1.0	1.0	1.5
Clerical	23.8	22.8	20.2	27.9	35.1	32.4
Operators	23.2	43.6	34.8	16.1	27.6	17.8
Total White Collar	67.6	69.9	77.5	70.0	78.0	77.6
Outside Crafts	21.0	18.6	15.7	19.6	12.8	15.4
Inside Crafts	9.8	3.7	5.6	8.8	4.7	6.6
Service Workers	1.6	7.8	1.2	1.6	4.5	0.4
Total Blue Collar	32.4	30.1	22.5	30.0	22.0	22.4
Total	100.0	100.0	100.0	100.0	100.0	100.0

TABLE V-A-30

AT&T, Percent Distribution by Sex and Occupational Group
East South Central Region, 1973 and 1979

Occupational Group	1973			1979		
	All Employees	Males	Females	All Employees	Males	Females
Officials and Managers	14.9	26.2	5.5	20.9	33.4	10.5
Administrative	5.0	2.4	7.3	4.1	0.5	7.0
Sales Workers	0.7	1.2	0.3	1.0	1.2	0.7
Clerical	23.8	1.5	42.3	27.9	4.7	47.2
Operators	23.2	2.0	40.8	16.1	2.0	27.9
Total White Collar	67.6	33.3	96.2	70.0	41.8	93.3
Outside Crafts	21.0	46.0	0.2	19.6	40.8	2.0
Inside Crafts	9.8	17.8	3.2	8.8	14.9	3.9
Service Workers	1.6	2.9	0.4	1.6	2.5	0.8
Total Blue Collar	32.4	66.7	3.8	30.0	58.2	6.7
Total	100.0	100.0	100.0	100.0	100.0	100.0

TABLE V-A-31

AT&T, Male Employment by Race and Occupational Group
West North Central Region, 1973 and 1979

Occupational Group	1973						
	Male	Percent Male	Black	Percent Black	Other Minorities	Percent Other Minorities
Officials and Managers	4,358	73.0	42	1.0	9	0.2
Administrative	5	1.3	1	20.0	0	0.0
Sales Workers	273	58.7	8	2.9	4	1.5
Clerical	354	4.9	18	5.1	12	3.4
Operators	237	4.6	15	6.3	8	3.4
Total White Collar	5,227	27.1	84	1.6	33	0.6
Outside Crafts	4,791	98.1	79	1.6	80	1.7
Inside Crafts	2,265	92.6	23	1.0	13	0.6
Service Workers	572	70.4	70	12.2	19	3.3
Total Blue Collar	7,628	93.7	172	2.3	112	1.5
Total	12,855	46.9	256	2.0	145	1.1

	Male	Percent Male	Black	Percent Black	Other Minorities	Percent Other Minorities
			1979			
Officials and Managers	5,000	67.7	74	1.5	38	0.8
Administrative	36	8.4	0	0.0	1	2.8
Sales Workers	197	63.1	9	4.6	0	0.0
Clerical	882	10.6	31	3.5	15	1.7
Operators	360	8.5	13	3.6	10	2.8
Total White Collar	6,475	31.3	127	2.0	64	1.0
Outside Crafts	4,460	92.6	70	1.6	80	1.8
Inside Crafts	2,408	38.3	30	1.2	22	0.9
Service Workers	245	17.9	33	13.5	15	6.1
Total Blue Collar	7,113	37.7	133	1.9	117	1.6
Total	13,588	47.2	260	1.9	181	1.3

TABLE V-A-32

AT&T, Female Employment by Race and Occupational Group
West North Central Region, 1973 and 1979

			1973			
Occupational Group	Female	Percent Female	Black	Percent Black	Other Minorities	Percent Other Minorities
Officials and Managers	1,611	27.0	42	2.6	9	0.6
Administrative	381	98.7	11	2.9	1	0.3
Sales Workers	192	41.3	3	1.6	1	0.5
Clerical	6,903	95.1	241	3.5	91	1.3
Operators	4,961	95.4	127	2.6	51	1.1
Total White Collar	14,048	72.9	424	3.0	153	1.1
Outside Crafts	91	1.9	1	1.1	0	0.0
Inside Crafts	182	7.4	5	2.7	1	0.5
Service Workers	241	29.6	16	6.6	2	0.8
Total Blue Collar	514	6.3	22	4.3	3	0.6
Total	14,562	53.1	446	3.1	156	1.1

	Female	Percent Female	Black	Percent Black	Other Minorities	Percent Other Minorities
			1979			
Officials and Managers	2,381	32.3	82	3.4	16	0.7
Administrative	392	91.6	13	3.3	0	0.0
Sales Workers	115	36.9	6	5.2	0	0.0
Clerical	7,459	89.4	257	3.4	137	1.8
Operators	3,863	91.5	97	2.5	48	1.2
Total White Collar	14,210	68.7	455	3.2	201	1.4
Outside Crafts	359	7.4	5	.4	5	1.4
Inside Crafts	374	13.7	11	2.9	2	0.5
Service Workers	267	52.1	14	5.2	5	1.9
Total Blue Collar	1,000	12.3	30	3.0	12	1.2
Total	15,210	52.8	485	3.2	213	1.4

TABLE V-A-33
AT&T, Employment by Race and Occupational Group
West North Central Region, 1973 and 1979

			1973		
Occupational Group	Total	Black	Percent Black	Other Minorities	Percent Other Minorities
Officials and Managers	5,969	89	1.4	18	0.3
Administrative	386	12	3.1	1	0.3
Sales Workers	465	11	2.4	5	1.1
Clerical	7,257	259	3.6	103	1.4
Operators	5,198	142	2.7	59	1.1
Total White Collar	19,275	508	2.6	186	1.0
Outside Crafts	4,882	80	1.6	80	1.6
Inside Crafts	2,447	28	1.1	14	0.6
Service Workers	813	86	10.6	21	2.6
Total Blue Collar	8,142	194	2.4	115	1.4
Total	27,417	702	2.6	301	1.1

	Total	Black	1979 Percent Black	Other Minorities	Percent Other Minorities
Officials and Managers	7,381	156	2.1	54	0.7
Administrative	428	13	3.0	1	0.2
Sales Workers	312	15	4.8	0	0.0
Clerical	8,341	288	3.5	152	1.8
Operators	4,223	110	2.6	58	1.4
Total White Collar	20,685	582	2.8	265	1.3
Outside Crafts	4,819	75	1.6	85	1.8
Inside Crafts	2,782	41	1.5	24	0.9
Service Workers	512	47	9.2	20	3.9
Total Blue Collar	8,113	163	2.0	129	1.6
Total	28,798	745	2.6	394	1.4

TABLE V-A-34

AT&T, Employment by Sex and Occupational Group
West North Central Region, 1973 and 1979

Occupational Group	Total	Male	1973 Percent Male	Female	Percent Female
Officials and Managers	5,969	4,358	73.0	1,611	27.0
Administrative	386	5	1.3	381	98.7
Sales Workers	465	273	58.7	192	41.3
Clerical	7,257	354	4.9	6,903	95.1
Operators	5,198	237	4.6	4,961	95.4
Total White Collar	19,275	5,227	27.1	14,048	72.9
Outside Crafts	4,882	4,791	98.1	91	1.9
Inside Crafts	2,447	2,265	92.6	182	7.4
Service Workers	813	572	70.4	241	29.6
Total Blue Collar	8,142	7,628	93.7	514	6.3
Total	27,417	12,855	46.9	14,562	53.1

		1979		
	Total	Male	Percent Male	Female	Percent Female
Officials and Managers	7,381	5,000	67.7	2,381	32.3
Administrative	428	36	8.4	392	91.6
Sales Workers	312	197	63.1	115	36.9
Clerical	8,341	882	10.6	7,459	89.4
Operators	4,223	360	8.5	3,863	91.5
Total White Collar	20,685	6,475	31.3	14,210	68.7
Outside Crafts	4,819	4,460	92.6	359	7.4
Inside Crafts	2,782	2,408	88.3	374	13.7
Service Workers	512	245	47.9	267	52.1
Total Blue Collar	8,113	7,113	87.7	1,000	12.3
Total	28,798	13,588	47.2	15,210	52.8

TABLE V-A-35

AT&T, Percent Distribution by Race and Occupational Group
West North Central Region, 1973 and 1979

Occupational Group	1973			1979		
	All Employees	Blacks	Other Minorities	All Employees	Blacks	Other Minorities
Officials and Managers	21.8	11.9	6.0	25.6	20.9	13.7
Administrative	1.4	1.7	0.3	1.5	1.7	0.3
Sales Workers	1.7	1.6	1.7	1.1	2.0	0.0
Clerical	26.5	36.9	34.3	29.0	38.7	38.6
Operators	19.0	20.3	19.6	14.7	14.8	14.7
Total White Collar	70.4	72.4	61.9	71.9	78.1	67.3
Outside Crafts	17.8	11.4	26.6	16.7	10.1	21.6
Inside Crafts	8.9	4.0	4.7	9.7	5.5	6.1
Service Workers	2.9	12.2	6.8	1.7	6.3	5.0
Total Blue Collar	29.6	27.6	38.1	28.1	21.9	32.7
Total	100.0	100.0	100.0	100.0	100.0	100.0

TABLE V-A-36
AT&T, Percent Distribution by Sex and Occupational Group
West North Central Region, 1973 and 1979

Occupational Group	1973			1979		
	All Employees	Males	Females	All Employees	Males	Females
Officials and Managers	21.8	35.9	11.1	25.6	36.8	15.7
Administrative	1.4	0.0	2.6	1.5	0.3	2.6
Sales Workers	1.7	2.1	1.3	1.1	1.4	0.8
Clerical	26.5	2.3	47.4	29.0	6.5	49.0
Operators	19.0	1.3	34.1	14.7	2.6	25.4
Total White Collar	70.4	40.6	96.5	71.9	47.6	93.5
Outside Crafts	17.8	37.3	0.6	16.7	32.8	2.4
Inside Crafts	8.9	17.6	1.2	9.7	17.7	2.5
Service Workers	2.9	4.5	1.7	1.7	1.9	1.6
Total Blue Collar	29.6	59.4	3.5	28.1	52.4	6.5
Total	100.0	100.0	100.0	100.0	100.0	100.0

TABLE V-A-37

AT&T, Male Employment by Race and Occupational Group
West South Central Region, 1973 and 1979

Occupational Group	1973					
	Male	Percent Male	Black	Percent Black	Other Minorities	Percent Other Minorities
Officials and Managers	7,319	68.8	96	1.3	157	2.1
Administrative	1,850	50.5	68	3.7	74	4.0
Sales Workers	864	60.9	43	5.0	53	6.1
Clerical	853	4.7	83	9.7	88	10.3
Operators	734	4.2	67	9.1	79	10.8
Total White Collar	11,620	22.7	357	3.1	451	3.9
Outside Crafts	13,453	99.1	584	4.3	743	5.5
Inside Crafts	7,686	88.2	439	5.7	323	4.2
Service Workers	914	78.4	429	46.9	88	9.6
Total Blue Collar	22,053	94.0	1,452	6.6	1,154	5.2
Total	33,673	45.2	1,809	5.4	1,605	4.8

	1979					
	Male	Percent Male	Black	Percent Black	Other Minorities	Percent Other Minorities
Officials and Managers	9,760	66.8	438	4.5	562	5.8
Administrative	3,212	48.8	211	6.6	202	6.3
Sales Workers	1,255	47.8	124	9.9	114	9.1
Clerical	2,912	11.4	476	16.3	364	12.5
Operators	1,018	8.2	145	14.2	185	18.2
Total White Collar	18,157	29.4	1,394	7.7	1,427	7.9
Outside Crafts	15,177	94.0	928	5.1	1,324	8.7
Inside Crafts	6,768	72.9	462	3.8	398	5.9
Service Workers	78	55.7	54	69.2	8	10.3
Total Blue Collar	22,023	36.1	1,444	6.6	1,730	7.9
Total	40,180	46.0	2,838	7.1	3,157	7.9

TABLE V-A-38

AT&T, Female Employment by Race and Occupational Group
West South Central Region, 1973 and 1979

Occupational Group	1973					
	Female	Percent Female	Black	Percent Black	Other Minorities	Percent Other Minorities
Officials and Managers	3,316	31.2	140	4.2	124	3.7
Administrative	1,813	49.5	84	4.6	67	3.7
Sales Workers	554	39.1	51	9.2	28	5.1
Clerical	17,105	95.3	1,846	10.8	1,157	6.8
Operators	16,683	95.8	2,763	16.6	1,203	7.2
Total White Collar	39,471	77.3	4,884	12.4	2,579	6.5
Outside Crafts	123	0.9	3	2.4	3	2.4
Inside Crafts	1,027	11.8	75	7.3	52	5.1
Service Workers	252	21.6	92	36.5	13	5.2
Total Blue Collar	1,402	6.0	170	12.1	68	4.9
Total	40,873	54.8	5,054	12.4	2,647	6.5

	Female	Percent Female	Black	Percent Black	Other Minorities	Percent Other Minorities
			1979			
Officials and Managers	4,855	33.2	486	10.0	305	6.3
Administrative	3,365	51.2	523	15.5	319	9.5
Sales Workers	1,368	52.2	271	19.8	97	7.1
Clerical	22,537	88.6	3,605	16.0	2,377	10.5
Operators	11,424	91.8	2,061	18.0	1,115	9.8
Total White Collar	43,543	70.6	6,946	15.9	4,213	9.7
Outside Crafts	963	6.0	110	11.4	85	8.8
Inside Crafts	2,520	27.1	274	10.9	210	8.3
Service Workers	62	44.3	36	58.1	2	3.2
Total Blue Collar	3,550	13.9	420	11.8	297	8.4
Total	47,099	54.0	7,366	15.6	4,510	9.6

TABLE V-A-39

AT&T, Employment by Race and Occupational Group
West South Central Region, 1973 and 1979

Occupational Group	Total	1973 Black	1973 Percent Black	1973 Other Minorities	1973 Percent Other Minorities
Officials and Managers	10,635	236	2.2	281	2.6
Administrative	3,663	152	4.1	141	3.8
Sales Workers	1,418	94	6.6	81	5.7
Clerical	17,958	1,929	10.7	1,245	6.9
Operators	17,417	2,830	16.2	1,282	7.4
Total White Collar	51,091	5,241	10.3	3,030	5.9
Outside Crafts	13,576	587	4.3	746	5.5
Inside Crafts	8,713	514	5.9	375	4.3
Service Workers	1,166	521	44.7	101	8.7
Total Blue Collar	23,455	1,622	6.9	1,222	5.2
Total	74,546	6,863	9.2	4,252	5.7

	Total	Black	1979 Percent Black	Other Minorities	Percent Other Minorities
Officials and Managers	14,615	924	6.3	867	5.9
Administrative	6,557	734	11.2	521	7.9
Sales Workers	2,623	395	15.1	211	8.0
Clerical	25,499	4,081	16.0	2,741	10.8
Operators	12,442	2,206	17.7	1,300	10.4
Total White Collar	61,706	8,340	13.5	5,640	9.1
Outside Crafts	16,145	1,038	6.4	1,409	8.7
Inside Crafts	9,288	736	7.9	608	6.5
Service Workers	140	90	64.3	10	7.1
Total Blue Collar	25,573	1,864	7.3	2,027	7.9
Total	87,279	10,204	11.7	7,667	8.8

TABLE V-A-40

AT&T, Employment by Sex and Occupational Group
West South Central Region, 1973 and 1979

Occupational Group	Total	1973 Male	Percent Male	Female	Percent Female
Officials and Managers	10,365	7,139	68.8	3,316	31.2
Administrative	3,663	1,850	50.5	1,813	49.5
Sales Workers	1,418	864	60.9	554	39.1
Clerical	17,958	853	4.7	17,105	95.3
Operators	17,417	734	4.2	16,683	95.8
Total White Collar	51,091	11,620	22.7	39,471	77.3
Outside Crafts	13,576	13,453	99.1	123	0.9
Inside Crafts	8,713	7,686	88.2	1,027	11.8
Service Workers	1,166	914	78.4	252	21.6
Total Blue Collar	23,455	22,053	94.0	1,402	6.0
Total	74,546	33,673	45.2	40,873	54.8

		1979			
	Total	Male	Percent Male	Female	Percent Female
Officials and Managers	14,615	9,760	66.8	4,855	33.2
Administrative	6,577	3,212	48.8	3,365	51.2
Sales Workers	2,623	1,255	47.8	1,368	52.2
Clerical	25,449	2,912	11.4	22,537	88.6
Operators	12,442	1,018	8.2	11,424	91.8
Total White Collar	61,706	18,157	29.4	43,549	70.6
Outside Crafts	16,145	15,177	94.0	968	6.0
Inside Crafts	9,288	6,768	72.9	2,520	27.1
Service Workers	140	78	55.7	62	44.3
Total Blue Collar	25,573	22,023	86.1	3,550	13.9
Total	87,279	40,180	46.0	47,099	54.0

TABLE V-A-41
AT&T, Percent Distribution by Race and Occupational Group
West South Central Region, 1973 and 1979

Occupational Group	1973			1979		
	All Employees	Blacks	Other Minorities	All Employees	Blacks	Other Minorities
Officials and Managers	14.3	3.4	6.6	16.7	9.1	11.3
Administrative	4.9	2.2	3.3	7.5	7.2	6.8
Sales Workers	1.9	1.4	1.9	3.0	3.9	2.8
Clerical	24.1	28.1	29.3	29.2	40.0	35.8
Operators	23.4	41.2	30.2	14.3	21.6	17.0
Total White Collar	68.6	76.3	71.3	70.7	81.8	73.7
Outside Crafts	18.2	8.6	17.5	18.5	10.2	18.4
Inside Crafts	11.7	7.5	8.9	10.6	7.2	7.8
Service Workers	1.5	7.6	2.3	0.2	0.8	0.1
Total Blue Collar	31.4	23.7	28.7	29.3	18.2	26.3
Total	100.0	100.0	100.0	100.0	100.0	100.0

TABLE V-A-42

AT&T, Percent Distribution by Sex and Occupational Group
West South Central Region, 1973 and 1979

Occupational Group	1973			1979		
	All Employees	Males	Females	All Employees	Males	Females
Officials and Managers	14.3	21.8	8.1	16.7	24.3	10.3
Administrative	4.9	5.5	4.4	7.5	8.0	7.1
Sales Workers	1.9	2.6	1.4	3.0	3.1	2.9
Clerical	24.1	2.5	41.8	29.2	7.2	47.9
Operators	23.4	2.2	40.8	14.3	2.5	24.3
Total White Collar	68.6	34.6	96.5	70.7	45.1	92.5
Outside Crafts	18.2	40.0	0.3	18.5	37.8	2.0
Inside Crafts	11.7	22.8	2.5	10.6	16.8	5.4
Service Workers	1.5	2.6	0.7	0.2	0.3	0.1
Total Blue Collar	31.4	65.4	3.5	29.3	54.9	7.5
Total	100.0	100.0	100.0	100.0	100.0	100.0

TABLE V-A-43

AT&T, Male Employment by Race and Occupational Group
Mountain Region, 1973 and 1979

Occupational Group	Male	Percent Male	1973 Black	Percent Black	Hispanic	Percent Hispanic	Other Minorities	Percent Other Minorities
Officials and Managers	6,298	75.3	42	0.7	125	2.0	33	0.5
Administrative	16	3.7	6	37.5	1	6.3	0	0.0
Sales Workers	212	56.8	8	3.8	12	5.7	0	0.0
Clerical	846	7.9	41	4.8	117	13.8	10	1.2
Operators	523	6.6	23	4.4	84	16.1	8	1.5
Total White Collar	7,895	28.4	120	1.5	339	4.3	51	0.6
Outside Crafts	6,803	93.3	115	1.7	776	11.3	81	1.2
Inside Crafts	3,552	86.5	55	1.5	269	7.6	43	1.2
Service Workers	901	79.5	87	9.7	177	19.6	20	2.2
Total Blue Collar	11,256	93.1	257	2.3	1,212	10.8	144	1.3
Total	19,151	48.0	377	2.0	1,551	8.1	195	1.0

	Male	Percent Male	Black	Percent Black	1979 Hispanic	Percent Hispanic	Other Minorities	Percent Other Minorities
Officials and Managers	7,732	67.2	85	1.1	392	5.1	85	1.1
Administrative	76	17.1	5	6.6	8	10.5	2	2.6
Sales Workers	184	43.2	8	4.3	17	9.2	2	1.1
Clerical	2,085	14.5	85	4.1	362	17.4	30	1.4
Operators	671	11.0	23	3.4	109	16.2	11	1.6
Total White Collar	10,748	32.7	207	1.9	888	8.3	130	1.2
Outside Crafts	6,524	92.4	86	1.3	657	10.1	88	1.3
Inside Crafts	3,470	73.4	56	1.6	253	7.3	40	1.2
Service Workers	522	51.0	55	10.5	106	20.3	13	2.5
Total Blue Collar	10,516	82.0	197	1.9	1,016	9.7	141	1.3
Total	21,264	46.6	404	1.9	1,904	9.0	271	1.3

TABLE V-A-44

AT&T, Female Employment by Race and Occupational Group
Mountain Region, 1973 and 1979

Occupational Group	Female	Percent Female	Black	Percent Black	Hispanic	Percent Hispanic	Other Minorities	Percent Other Minorities
					1973			
Officials and Managers	2,067	24.7	50	2.4	84	4.1	17	0.8
Administrative	418	96.3	2	0.5	13	3.1	1	0.2
Sales Workers	161	43.2	6	3.7	8	5.0	3	1.9
Clerical	9,844	92.1	402	4.1	1,219	12.4	148	1.5
Operators	7,428	93.4	328	4.4	1,091	14.7	87	1.2
Total White Collar	19,918	71.6	788	4.0	2,415	12.1	256	1.3
Outside Crafts	46	0.7	1	2.2	5	10.9	0	0.0
Inside Crafts	555	13.5	9	1.6	44	7.9	4	0.7
Service Workers	232	20.5	41	17.7	39	16.8	1	0.4
Total Blue Collar	833	6.9	51	6.1	88	10.6	5	0.6
Total	20,751	52.0	839	4.0	2,503	12.1	261	1.3

					1979			
	Female	Percent Female	Black	Percent Black	Hispanic	Percent Hispanic	Other Minorities	Percent Other Minorities
Officials and Managers	3,775	32.8	109	2.9	350	9.3	51	1.4
Administrative	369	82.9	9	2.4	27	7.3	10	2.7
Sales Workers	242	56.8	8	3.3	25	10.3	0	0.0
Clerical	12,269	85.5	555	4.5	1,750	14.3	223	1.8
Operators	5,429	82.0	251	4.6	784	14.4	96	1.8
Total White Collar	22,084	67.3	932	4.2	2,936	13.3	380	1.7
Outside Crafts	540	7.6	10	1.9	55	10.2	7	1.3
Inside Crafts	1,260	26.6	32	2.5	134	10.6	11	0.9
Service Workers	502	49.0	39	7.8	87	17.3	11	2.2
Total Blue Collar	2,302	18.0	81	3.5	276	12.0	29	1.3
Total	24,386	53.4	1,013	4.2	3,212	13.2	409	1.7

TABLE V-A-45

AT&T, Employment by Race and Occupational Group
Mountain Region, 1973 and 1979

Occupational Group	Total	1973 Black	Percent Black	Hispanic	Percent Hispanic	Other Minorities	Percent Other Minorities
Officials and Managers	8,365	92	1.1	209	2.5	50	0.6
Administrative	434	8	1.8	14	3.2	1	0.2
Sales Workers	373	14	3.8	20	5.4	3	0.8
Clerical	10,690	443	4.1	1,336	12.5	158	1.5
Operators	7,951	351	4.4	1,175	14.8	95	1.2
Total White Collar	27,813	908	3.3	2,754	9.9	307	1.1
Outside Crafts	6,849	116	1.7	771	11.3	81	1.2
Inside Crafts	4,107	64	1.6	313	7.6	47	1.1
Service Workers	1,133	128	11.3	216	19.1	21	1.9
Total Blue Collar	12,089	308	2.5	1,300	10.8	149	1.2
Total	39,902	1,216	3.0	4,054	10.2	456	1.1

| | 1979 | | | | | | |
	Total	Black	Percent Black	Hispanic	Percent Hispanic	Other Minorities	Percent Other Minorities
Officials and Managers	11,507	195	1.7	742	6.4	136	1.2
Administrative	445	14	3.1	35	7.9	12	2.7
Sales Workers	426	16	3.8	42	9.9	2	0.5
Clerical	14,354	640	4.5	2,112	14.7	253	1.8
Operators	6,100	274	4.5	893	14.6	107	1.8
Total White Collar	32,832	1,139	3.5	3,824	11.6	510	1.6
Outside Crafts	7,064	96	1.4	712	10.1	95	1.3
Inside Crafts	4,730	88	1.9	387	8.2	51	1.1
Service Workers	1,024	94	9.2	193	18.8	24	2.3
Total Blue Collar	12,818	278	2.2	1,292	10.1	170	1.3
Total	45,650	1,417	3.1	5,116	11.2	680	1.5

TABLE V-A-46

AT&T, Employment by Sex and Occupational Group
Mountain Region, 1973 and 1979

Occupational Group	Total	Male	Percent Male	Female	Percent Female
			1973		
Officials and Managers	8,365	6,298	75.3	2,067	24.7
Administrative	434	16	3.7	418	96.3
Sales Workers	373	212	56.8	161	43.2
Clerical	10,690	846	7.9	9,844	92.1
Operators	7,951	523	6.6	7,428	93.4
Total White Collar	27,813	7,895	28.4	19,918	71.6
Outside Crafts	6,849	6,803	93.3	46	0.7
Inside Crafts	4,107	3,552	86.5	555	13.5
Service Workers	1,133	901	79.5	232	20.5
Total Blue Collar	12,089	11,256	93.1	833	6.9
Total	39,902	19,151	48.0	20,751	52.0

	Total		1979		
	Total	Male	Percent Male	Female	Percent Female
Officials and Managers	11,507	7,732	67.2	3,775	32.8
Administrative	445	76	17.1	369	82.9
Sales Workers	426	184	43.2	242	56.8
Clerical	14,354	2,085	14.5	12,269	85.5
Operators	6,100	671	11.0	5,429	89.0
Total White Collar	32,832	10,743	32.7	22,084	67.3
Outside Crafts	7,064	6,524	92.4	540	7.6
Inside Crafts	4,730	3,470	73.4	1,260	26.6
Service Workers	1,024	522	51.0	502	49.0
Total Blue Collar	12,818	10,516	82.0	2,302	18.0
Total	45,650	21,264	46.6	24,386	53.4

TABLE V-A-47

AT&T, Percent Distribution by Race and Occupational Group
Mountain Region, 1973 and 1979

Occupational Group	1973				1979			
	All Employees	Blacks	Hispanics	Other Minorities	All Employees	Blacks	Hispanics	Other Minorities
Officials and Managers	21.0	7.4	5.1	11.7	25.2	13.8	14.5	20.0
Administrative	1.1	0.7	0.3	0.2	1.0	1.0	0.7	1.8
Sales Workers	0.9	1.2	0.5	0.7	0.9	1.1	0.8	0.3
Clerical	26.8	36.5	33.0	34.3	31.4	45.2	41.3	37.2
Operators	19.9	28.9	29.0	20.7	13.4	19.3	17.5	15.7
Total White Collar	69.7	74.7	67.9	67.6	71.9	80.4	74.8	75.0
Outside Crafts	17.2	9.6	19.0	17.6	15.5	6.8	13.9	14.0
Inside Crafts	10.3	5.3	7.7	10.2	10.4	6.2	7.6	7.5
Service Workers	2.8	10.4	5.4	4.6	2.2	6.6	3.7	3.5
Total Blue Collar	30.3	25.3	32.1	32.4	28.1	19.6	25.2	25.0
Total	100.0	100.0	100.0	100.0	100.0	100.0	100.0	100.0

TABLE V-A-48

AT&T, Percent Distribution by Sex and Occupational Group Mountain Region, 1973 and 1979

Occupational Group	1973			1979		
	All Employees	Males	Females	All Employees	Males	Females
Officials and Managers	21.0	22.9	10.0	25.2	36.4	15.5
Administrative	1.1	0.1	2.0	1.0	0.4	1.5
Sales Workers	0.9	1.1	0.8	0.9	0.9	1.0
Clerical	26.8	4.4	47.4	31.4	9.8	50.3
Operators	19.9	2.7	35.8	13.4	3.2	22.3
Total White Collar	69.7	41.2	96.0	71.9	50.7	90.6
Outside Crafts	17.2	35.5	0.2	15.5	30.7	2.2
Inside Crafts	10.3	18.6	2.7	10.4	16.3	5.2
Service Workers	2.8	4.7	1.1	2.2	2.3	2.0
Total Blue Collar	30.3	58.8	4.0	28.1	49.3	9.4
Total	100.0	100.0	100.0	100.0	100.0	100.0

TABLE V-A-49
AT&T, Male Employment by Race and Occupational Group
Pacific Region, 1973 and 1979

Occupational Group	Male	Percent Male	1973 Black	Percent Black	Hispanic	Percent Hispanic	Other Minorities	Percent Other Minorities
Officials and Managers	17,936	69.8	257	1.4	386	2.2	224	1.2
Administrative	36	2.8	2	5.6	0	0.0	2	5.6
Sales Workers	370	42.0	30	8.1	10	2.7	3	0.8
Clerical	2,542	7.3	233	9.2	396	15.6	326	12.8
Operators	1,370	6.9	147	10.7	271	19.7	48	3.5
Total White Collar	22,254	27.0	669	3.0	1,063	4.8	603	2.7
Outside Crafts	16,176	98.5	696	4.3	1,263	7.8	312	1.9
Inside Crafts	11,779	86.5	566	4.8	834	7.1	404	3.4
Service Workers	2,075	75.0	255	12.3	332	16.0	154	7.4
Total Blue Collar	30,030	91.6	1,517	5.1	2,429	8.1	870	2.9
Total	52,284	45.4	2,186	4.2	3,492	6.7	1,473	2.8

1979

	Male	Percent Male	Black	Percent Black	Hispanic	Percent Hispanic	Other Minorities	Percent Other Minorities
Officials and Managers	18,671	64.2	560	3.0	972	5.2	465	2.5
Administrative	230	16.5	12	5.2	9	3.9	12	5.2
Sales Workers	364	55.1	28	7.7	18	4.9	4	1.1
Clerical	5,276	13.1	463	3.8	708	13.4	523	9.9
Operators	2,159	12.1	216	10.0	280	13.0	134	6.2
Total White Collar	26,700	29.9	1,279	4.8	1,987	7.4	1,138	4.3
Outside Crafts	17,558	90.8	818	4.7	1,703	9.7	555	3.2
Inside Crafts	10,525	74.4	611	5.8	923	8.8	493	4.7
Service Workers	416	52.6	88	21.2	121	29.1	68	16.3
Total Blue Collar	28,499	83.2	1,517	5.3	2,747	9.6	1,116	3.9
Total	55,199	44.6	2,796	5.1	4,734	8.6	2,254	4.1

TABLE V-A-50

AT&T, Female Employment by Race and Occupational Group
Pacific Region, 1973 and 1979

Occupational Group	Female	Percent Female	1973					
			Black	Percent Black	Hispanic	Percent Hispanic	Other Minorities	Percent Other Minorities
Officials and Managers	7,768	30.2	406	5.2	285	3.7	193	2.5
Administrative	1,234	97.2	54	4.4	43	3.5	46	3.7
Sales Workers	510	58.0	35	6.9	17	3.3	19	3.7
Clerical	32,160	92.7	4,091	12.7	2,908	9.0	1,853	5.8
Operators	18,438	93.1	2,256	12.2	1,664	9.0	420	2.3
Total White Collar	60,110	73.0	6,842	11.4	4,917	8.2	2,531	4.2
Outside Crafts	244	1.5	16	6.6	17	7.0	8	3.3
Inside Crafts	1,831	13.5	180	9.8	108	5.9	49	2.7
Service Workers	691	25.0	124	17.9	63	9.1	25	3.6
Total Blue Collar	2,766	8.4	320	11.6	188	6.8	82	3.0
Total	62,876	54.6	7,162	11.4	5,105	8.1	2,613	4.2

	Female	Percent Female	Black	Percent Black	1979 Hispanic	Percent Hispanic	Other Minorities	Percent Other Minorities
Officials and Managers	10,410	35.8	806	7.7	674	6.5	428	4.1
Administrative	1,161	83.5	63	5.4	68	5.9	66	5.7
Sales Workers	297	44.9	34	11.4	16	5.4	9	3.0
Clerical	35,151	86.9	4,922	14.0	3,798	10.8	2,634	7.5
Operators	15,651	87.9	1,537	10.5	1,664	10.6	558	3.6
Total White Collar	62,670	70.1	7,462	11.9	6,220	9.9	3,695	5.9
Outside Crafts	1,776	9.2	122	6.9	173	9.7	64	3.6
Inside Crafts	3,618	25.6	515	14.2	343	9.5	205	5.7
Service Workers	375	47.4	87	23.2	65	17.3	13	3.5
Total Blue Collar	5,769	16.8	724	12.5	581	10.1	282	4.9
Total	68,439	55.4	8,186	12.0	6,801	9.9	3,977	5.8

TABLE V-A-51
AT&T, Employment by Race and Occupational Group
Pacific Region, 1973 and 1979

Occupational Group	1973							
	Total	Black	Percent Black	Hispanic	Percent Hispanic	Other Minorities	Percent Other Minorities
Officials and Managers	25,704	663	2.6	671	2.6	417	1.6
Administrative	1,270	56	4.4	43	3.4	48	3.8
Sales Workers	880	65	7.4	27	3.1	22	2.5
Clerical	34,702	4,324	12.5	3,304	9.5	2,179	6.3
Operators	19,808	2,403	12.1	1,935	9.8	468	2.4
Total White Collar	82,364	7,511	9.1	5,980	7.3	3,134	3.8
Outside Crafts	16,420	712	4.3	1,280	7.8	320	1.9
Inside Crafts	13,610	746	5.5	942	6.9	453	3.3
Service Workers	2,766	379	13.7	395	14.3	179	6.5
Total Blue Collar	32,796	1,837	5.6	2,617	8.0	952	2.9
Total	115,160	9,348	8.1	8,597	7.5	4,086	3.5

				1979			
	Total	Black	Percent Black	Hispanic	Percent Hispanic	Other Minorities	Percent Other Minorities
Officials and Managers	29,081	1,366	4.7	1,646	5.7	893	3.1
Administrative	1,391	75	5.4	77	5.5	78	5.6
Sales Workers	661	62	9.4	34	5.1	13	2.0
Clerical	40,427	5,335	13.3	4,506	11.1	3,157	7.8
Operators	17,810	1,853	10.4	1,944	10.9	692	3.9
Total White Collar	89,370	8,741	9.8	8,207	9.2	4,833	5.4
Outside Crafts	19,334	940	4.9	1,876	9.7	619	3.2
Inside Crafts	14,143	1,126	8.0	1,266	9.0	698	4.9
Service Workers	791	175	22.1	186	23.5	81	10.2
Total Blue Collar	34,268	2,241	6.5	3,328	9.7	1,398	4.1
Total	123,638	10,982	8.9	11,535	9.3	6,231	9.3

TABLE V-A-52

AT&T, Employment by Sex and Occupational Group

Pacific Region, 1973 and 1979

Occupational Group	Total	1973 Male	Percent Male	Female	Percent Female
Officials and Managers	25,704	17,936	69.8	7,768	30.2
Administrative	1,270	36	2.8	1,234	97.2
Sales Workers	880	370	42.0	510	58.0
Clerical	34,702	2,542	7.3	32,160	92.7
Operators	19,808	1,370	6.9	18,438	93.1
Total White Collar	82,364	22,254	27.0	60,110	73.0
Outside Crafts	16,420	16,176	98.5	244	1.5
Inside Crafts	13,610	11,779	86.5	1,831	13.5
Service Workers	2,766	2,075	75.0	691	25.0
Total Blue Collar	32,796	30,030	91.6	2,766	8.4
Total	115,160	52,284	45.4	62,876	54.6

	Total	Male	1979 Percent Male	Female	Percent Female
Officials and Managers	29,081	18,671	64.2	10,410	35.8
Administrative	1,391	230	16.5	1,161	83.5
Sales Workers	661	364	55.1	297	44.9
Clerical	40,427	5,276	13.1	35,151	86.9
Operators	17,810	2,159	12.1	15,651	87.9
Total White Collar	89,370	26,700	29.9	62,670	70.1
Outside Crafts	19,334	17,558	90.8	1,776	9.2
Inside Crafts	14,143	10,525	74.4	3,618	25.6
Service Workers	791	416	52.6	375	47.4
Total Blue Collar	34,268	28,499	83.2	5,769	16.7
Total	123,638	55,199	44.6	68,439	55.4

TABLE V-A-53

AT&T, Percent Distribution by Race and Occupational Group
Pacific Region, 1973 and 1979

Occupational Group	1973				1979			
	All Employees	Blacks	Hispanics	Other Minorities	All Employees	Blacks	Hispanics	Other Minorities
Officials and Managers	22.3	7.1	7.8	10.2	23.5	9.8	9.9	10.8
Administrative	1.1	0.6	0.5	1.2	1.1	0.8	1.0	1.7
Sales Workers	0.8	0.7	0.3	0.6	0.5	0.4	0.2	0.2
Clerical	30.1	46.3	38.4	53.3	32.7	60.1	55.8	66.2
Operators	17.2	25.7	22.5	11.4	14.4	20.0	24.5	14.0
Total White Collar	71.5	80.4	69.5	76.7	72.2	91.1	91.4	92.9
Outside Crafts	14.3	7.6	14.9	7.9	15.6	1.5	2.5	1.6
Inside Crafts	11.8	8.0	10.9	11.1	11.4	6.3	5.0	5.2
Service Workers	2.4	4.0	4.7	4.3	0.8	1.1	1.1	0.3
Total Blue Collar	28.5	19.6	30.5	23.3	27.8	8.9	8.6	7.1
Total	100.0	100.0	100.0	100.0	100.0	100.0	100.0	100.0

TABLE V-A-54
AT&T, Percent Distribution by Sex and Occupational Group
Pacific Region, 1973 and 1979

Occupational Group	1973			1979		
	All Employees	Males	Females	All Employees	Males	Females
Officials and Managers	22.3	54.3	12.4	23.5	33.8	15.2
Administrative	1.1	0.1	2.0	1.1	0.4	1.7
Sales Workers	0.8	0.7	0.8	0.5	0.7	0.4
Clerical	30.1	4.9	51.-	32.7	9.6	51.4
Operators	17.2	2.6	29.3	14.4	3.9	22.9
Total White Collar	71.5	42.5	95.6	72.2	48.4	91.6
Outside Crafts	14.3	30.9	0.4	15.6	31.8	2.6
Inside Crafts	11.8	22.5	2.9	11.4	19.1	5.3
Service Workers	2.4	4.0	1.1	0.8	0.7	0.5
Total Blue Collar	28.5	57.4	4.4	27.8	51.6	8.4
Total	100.0	100.0	100.0	100.0	100.0	100.0

Appendix V-B

THE LOGIC OF COVARIANCE

Suppose we have two events, x and y, which occur simultaneously. Suppose further that x and y can each take on a total of n values. That is:

$$x = x_1, x_2, \ldots, x_n$$
$$y = y_1, y_2, \ldots, y_n$$

These values occur at random with probability $p(x_i, y_i)$ for i=1, 2, $\ldots$, n. Finally, assume we know the average value for x and the average value for y which we denote as m_x and m_y, respectively.

Given the above, we can consider the following formula:

$$COV_{xy} = \sum_{i=1}^{n} (x_i - m_x)(y_i - m_y)[p(x_i, y_i)]$$

We have two cases to examine. Case I: COV_{xy} is positive. In this situation our formula tells us that, on average, when x exceeds its mean value (m_x), y exceeds its mean value (m_y). Similarly, when x is below m_x, y, on average, is below m_y.

Comsider the following graph:

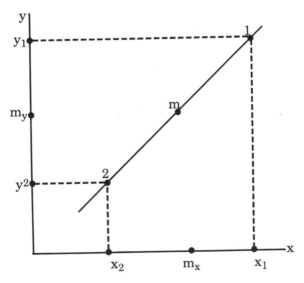

Point m corresponds to the joint location of the mean of x and the mean of y. Consider next point 1, associated with the simultaneous occurrence of the values x_1 and y_1. Both x and y values are in excess of their means. Point 2 contains the simultaneous occurrence of x and y values, both of which are below their means.

The graph depicts a situation of positive covariance. The upward slope of the line connecting the various points indicates the main implication of this—high values of x are associated with high values of y. The converse also holds—low values of x are associated with low values of y.

Case II: COV_{xy} is negative. In this situation, our formula states that, on average, when x exceeds its mean value, m_x, y is below m_y. Conversely, when y is above m_y, x is below m_x.

This situation is depicted in the following graph:

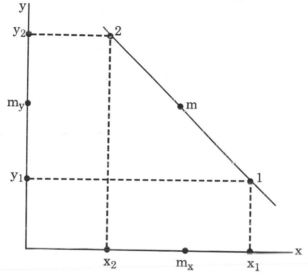

Point m again indicates the location of the joint mean of x and y. At point 1, x exceeds its mean value, but y is less than its mean. Point 2 presents the opposite result: y exceeds m_y, while x is below m_x.

The implication of the graph is that with negative covariance x and y move inversely. A large value of x implies a low value of y. The converse also holds. It is this inverse relationship that we have termed a tradeoff, and evidence of it is found in a negative covariance.

Application to the Analysis

Consider the case of white females and black males. We have nine geographical regions to examine (n=9). Nationwide, white female representation increased 2.4 percent (m_x=2.4) while the same figure for black males was 1.4 percent (m_y=1.4) (see Table III-1).

For management we obtain the following formula and result:

$$\sum_{i=1}^{9} (x_i - 2.4)(y_i - 1.4)[p(x_i, y_i)] = -1.1983$$

The negative covariance implies that, on average, large gains for white females are accompanied by small gains for black males and conversely. Thus, negative covariance is a sign of a tradeoff between the race-sex group within the occupational category considered. A further corollary is that the larger the absolute value of the negative covariance, the greater the degree of competition between the race-sex groups involved.

Appendix V-C

REGRESSION ANALYSIS
OF DETERMINANTS
OF REGIONAL EMPLOYMENT GAINS
OF MINORITIES

In this appendix, we provide statistical support for our statement that statistical parity, as opposed to economic variables, is the prime determinant of minority group advancement under the AT&T affirmative action program. Before presenting our results, however, we develop the logic underlying our approach.

If a prospective job applicant were to evaluate the advancement possibilities offered by a potential employer, he would consider several important aspects. Primary among these would be employee turnover, company profitability, and company growth prospects. For example, companies with high employee turnover rates will offer greater advancement prospects for workers who stay with the company than will similar firms that have lower employee turnover. Likewise, if a company is growing and profitable, we would expect it to offer greater advancement prospects than would be available at a stagnant firm.

It is just this form of reasoning that was used to analyze minority group gains in each of the nine census regions. Ideally, if economic variables were to determine the extent of minority group advances, we would expect that measures of profitability and company growth would play important roles in any statistical test conducted. If advancements of minority group workers were not determined by an economic motive but rather by a commitment to statistical parity, then an analysis of the data would show that the most significant variables governing minority advances would be employee turnover and the regional composition by race.

To conduct our test of the relative importance of the economic motive vis-à-vis the parity motive, a regression test was run for each minority race and sex group in management. Management was selected because it was the job category that offered the highest advancement potential during the period 1973–77. Two separate sets of tests (to be described below) were run for each minority race-sex group. Five variables were the basis of the analysis. For each variable we had nine observations—one for each census region. The five variables were:

Y = Percentage gain in a given minority race-sex group's representation in management.

X_1 = Percentage change in total operating company employment.

X_2 = Percentage change in total operating company earnings.

X_3 = Percentage change in total plant and equipment.

X_4 = Percentage of the population accounted for by the minority group being tested.

All data are in percentage terms and cover the period 1973 to 1977. Percentages were used to eliminate size differentials between regions. Were this not done, the results in New England, a relatively small region, would be dwarfed by a larger region such as the South Atlantic. The use of percentage figures eliminates this bias.

The percentage change in total employment was used as a proxy for turnover on the assumption (presumably valid) that large changes in employment are accompanied by high turnover. In addition, the change in the regional value of plant and equipment was used as a measure of growth.

Results of the Tests

Our first test involved simple one variable linear regression analysis. For each minority race-sex group variable, Y, the percentage change in that group's representation in management, was regressed on each of the remaining four variables separately. Thus, for each group four regressions were obtained of the form:

$$Y = a + bX \qquad\qquad i = 1,2,3,4.$$

The purpose of this test was to determine which single variable was the most important determinant of minority advances. To do this, R^2, the percentage of the total variation in minority group gains accounted for by the independent variable, was computed for each regression. Based on this we conclude that the single variable with the highest R^2 is the most important determinant of minority gains.

Table V-C-1 presents R^2 averaged over the six race-sex groups for each independent variable in the single regression test. (The reader is cautioned that the table presents the average results of the single variable test. Hence, the percentage figures when added together are not required to be less than 100 percent.)

These single variable regressions clearly demonstrate the importance of population representation in determining minority gains. By itself, regional population composition by race, on average, accounted for almost two-thirds of the variance in minority gains during the period of the consent decree. This percentage figure is more than three times that of any other variable in the table. This is consistent with our statement that statistical parity is the most significant determinant of the extent of minority group advances.

TABLE V-C-1
*Average Percent of Variation in Representation
Explained by Independent Variables*

Independent Variable	.	R^2
Change in Employment		18.0
Change in Earnings		15.3
Change in Plant and Equipment		15.7
Population Representation		65.5

Source: The Company.

The table further shows the subordinate role played by economic variables. To develop this further, a second set of tests was run in a multiple regression format. The equation estimated was of the form:

$$Y = a + b_1 X_1 + b_2 X_2 + b_3 X_3 + b_4 X_4$$

The variables in the above equation retain their previous definitions. This test was run for each minority race-sex group. T tests for significance were then conducted on the estimated coefficients. Our results are as follows:

1. The coefficient for population was significant in all but one case (Hispanic females). The T tests for this variable were the highest of the four independent variables analyzed. This lends further support for the results in Table V-C-1.

2. The coefficient of employment changes, b_1, was significant in three cases. The estimated coefficient for this variable was quite large, on average, indicating that areas with increasing employment offer significantly higher opportunities for minority managers.

3. The coefficient for earnings change was significant only in the case of blacks—both male and female. For no other race-sex group was profitability a significant factor in advancement.

4. The effect of growth on minority advances, as measured by b_3, was significant in only one case—and here it had a negative sign indicating that growth actually worked against the given race-sex group.

In short, our results offer ample support for the statement that regional population composition is the most important factor in minority gains under the affirmative action program at AT&T. The multiple regression analysis showed that regional employment growth was also a significant factor in minority progress. Economic variables, however, contribute little to explaining the gains experienced by these protected groups during the period 1973–77.

Our six regressions are summarized below. The values in parentheses under the coefficient estimate indicate that coefficient's T test score. Scores in excess of 2.2 indicate that the variable has a 95 percent probability of significantly affecting minority gains.

Black Males:

$$Y = 0.15 \quad + \; 11.72X_1 + \quad 0.05X_2 \quad -0.05X_3 \; +0.11X_4 \quad R^2 = 93.3$$
$$\; (2.4) \qquad\quad (2.5) \qquad (1.3) \qquad (5.5)$$

Black Females:

$$Y = 0.36 \quad + \; 9.13X_1 + \quad 0.03X_2 \quad -0.04X_3 \; +0.11X_4 \quad R^2 = 94.3$$
$$\; (2.2) \qquad\quad (3.0) \qquad (1.0) \qquad (5.5)$$

Hispanic Males:

$$Y = 1.01 \quad + \; 0.13X_1 \quad\; 0.02X_2 \quad +0.01X_3 \; +1.15X_4 \quad R^2 = 76.7$$
$$\; (0.02) \qquad\quad (1.0) \qquad (0.2) \qquad (2.2)$$

Hispanic Females:

$$Y = -0.14 - \; 3.43X_1 - \quad 0.03X_2 \quad +0.04X_3 \; +0.92X_4 \quad R^2 - 63.6$$
$$\; (0.6) \qquad\quad (1.5) \qquad (0.8) \qquad (1.8)$$

Other Minority Males:

$$Y = 0.48 \quad + \; 2.14X_1 + \quad 0.001X_2 \; -0.01X_3 \; +0.09X_4 \quad R^2 = 96.9$$
$$\; (3.6) \qquad\quad (0.5) \qquad (3.3) \qquad (9.0)$$

Other Minority Females:

$$Y = 0.22 \quad + \; 1.67X_1 + \quad 0.01X_2 \quad -0.01X_3 \; |\, 0.09X_4 \quad R^2 = 91.5$$
$$\; (1.9) \qquad\quad (1.8) \qquad (1.7) \qquad (4.5)$$

CHAPTER VI

The Question of Availability

The preceding chapters have been concerned chiefly with the effects of the implementation of the consent decree during the period 1973–79. Only in chapter II did we consider projections reaching beyond this time frame. In the present chapter the focus of the analysis shifts. We now examine an extremely important long-run implication of the consent decree—the question of availability.

THE CONCEPT OF AVAILABILITY

Availability as used here is both a demand and a supply concept. On the demand side, it refers to the mix of job openings and their geographic distribution that will occur in the foreseeable future. Under this concept of availability we consider such questions as the nature of the long-run employment prospects for telephone operators and data processors and the regional composition of employment; e.g., will the need for outside craft workers be greater in New England or in the Southwest during the next five years?

The other side of the availability issue is that of supply. It is perhaps this question, more than any other, that casts a serious pall over the ultimate long-run potential of the program induced by the AT&T consent decree. Specifically, once we have established the long-run projections for labor force demand, we must inquire whether there will be a sufficient supply of protected group workers to insure that all established targets will be attained. Obviously, public policy programs to insure increased opportunities for protected group workers will produce miminal results in the long run if there is an insufficient supply of workers to fill the targets or quotas.

The chapter begins with a consideration of the demand side of the labor market. Our results here derive from what we have already seen in chapter II. Future job openings in the Bell System will be increasingly technical in nature. These jobs will become concentrated in the Southwest and West, where both industry and the population are growing. Protected group workers, especially blacks, must attain greater technical skills and demonstrate a greater geographic mobility than at present if they are to continue their progress of previous years.

We then proceed to a discussion of the supply side of availability. Given the increasingly technical nature of the labor force, will a sufficient supply of qualified protected group workers be available to fill the new openings? Using a simulation model developed by the Wharton School's Industrial Research Unit, coupled with the logic of statistical parity, our analysis projects a serious long-run shortage of qualified protected group workers—even of white females.

In short, our results cast serious doubt on the efficacy of public policy programs to alter greatly the composition of the labor force during the next ten years. The dearth of qualified workers imposes a serious constraint on the efforts both of the private and the public sectors to increase substantially protected group employment in key skill areas. The opportunities may be there, but as our analysis shows, there is projected an insufficient supply of workers to take advantage of the increased openings.

AVAILABILITY—THE DEMAND SIDE

Our results from previous chapters indicate the increasingly technological nature of the AT&T labor force. In chapter II, we noted that the demand for managers skilled in the scientific and engineering disciplines has grown considerably. Applicants with technical backgrounds accounted for 45 percent of all new managerial hires in 1975.[1]

At the nonmanagerial level, this same trend is also observed. The demand for technicians skilled in operating and maintaining data processing and sophisticated computer systems has also increased. Meanwhile, nontechnical jobs, such as service workers and telephone operators, have experienced substantial reductions. These trends are predicted to continue.

In addition to the increasingly technical orientation of the labor force, another equally pronounced trend has begun to emerge—the shift of opportunities away from the industrial Northeast and Midwest and toward the "Sunbelt." The following excerpt from a study of the *New York Times* typifies this alteration in the geographic distribution of employment.

A substantial shift is under way at the American Telephone and

---

[1] AT&T, "EEO Reference Binder" (March 31, 1977), Section XIV, p. 1.

Telegraph Company, in effect, moving thousands of jobs from the East to the Sunbelt states.

This movement is taking place at the same time that the actual number of jobs in the Bell System, the nation's largest private employer, has been declining sharply. . . .

The projected declines in the East and growth in the Sunbelt are tied to Bell's own economic and marketing expectations.[2]

It should be noted, however, that these opportunity gains were not distributed uniformly throughout the Sunbelt. The Southeast, in particular, actually experienced a decline in its total labor force. New jobs in the Sunbelt were concentrated largely in the emerging areas of the Southwest and West; more specifically, in the West South Central, Mountain, and Pacific regions. This shift in opportunities is illustrated in Table VI-1, which gives the percentage of new openings in the Bell System that occurred in companies operating in these regions during the period of the consent decree. The table covers the five occupational groups upon which we have concentrated our analysis in the previous chapters.

Only in the sales worker category were employment gains in these two regions minimal. In the other four classifications, the concentration in job openings increased by at least 10 percent, with inside craft opportunities showing the largest rise.

The lesson of the above is clear. The opportunities for employment at AT&T are being increasingly concentrated in the Southwest and West. While operating companies outside this area are being forced to rely on attrition more and more as the sole source of new openings, the Sunbelt companies, fueled by an increasing growth rate in their areas, are offering a larger share of the new opportunities for Bell System employment.

What is the impact of this shift on the ability of AT&T significantly to alter its employment mix? Our previous results have shown a reluctance of minority group members, especially, to be geographically mobile within a given region. Given this, it is doubtful that many such workers will be willing to move to another region in order to gain employment at the Bell System.

There are high concentrations of blacks in the West South Central region, and Hispanics and other minority Americans have significant representation in both the Southwest and Pacific regions. Our projections augur well for individuals currently located in these regions. This, however, is of little concern to the many minority group members not fortunate enough to live in these

---

[2] Jerry M. Flint, "AT&T's Jobs Going from East to the Sunbelt," *New York Times*, August 9, 1977, pp. 43, 45.

TABLE VI-1

AT&T, Percentage of Total System Job Openings
Mountain, West South Central, and Pacific Regions, 1973–79

Occupational Group	1973	1979
Officials and Managers	25.4	38.5
Sales Workers	34.9	42.9
Outside Crafts	34.1	46.5
Inside Crafts	31.4	50.3
Clerical	34.9	45.6

Source: The Company.

regions. For them, the decision to work for AT&T will increasingly involve a choice between employment within their current region or a move to the West or Southwest. If past experience is any indication, it is doubtful that many will be willing to relocate.

AVAILABILITY—THE SUPPLY SIDE

More germane to the long-run effects of affirmative action is the question of the adequacy of the supply of protected group workers. Even abstracting from the problems raised by the geographic concentration of opportunities in the Sunbelt, more serious difficulties arise when one considers the potential availability of protected group workers with the proper technical and business backgrounds suitable for employment at the Bell System. If there is a noticeable dearth of qualified protected group workers, it makes little sense to require companies to fill targets or quotas.

To focus on this problem we make use of a simulation study conducted by Dr. Stephen A. Schneider of the Wharton School's Industrial Research Unit.[3] In his analysis, Dr. Schneider employed demographic and labor force data to simulate the supply of professional and managerial workers in four racial groups: white males and females, and black males and females. The study projected the labor supply for these four groups by occupation through 1985. Because of a lack of data, the simulation was not conducted for Hispanics or other minority groups. A short description of the Schneider methodology is given in Appendix VI-A.

To apply the Schneider study to the implementation of af-

---

[3] Stephen A. Schneider, *The Availability of Minorities and Women for Professional and Managerial Positions 1970–1985*, Manpower and Human Resources Studies No. 7 (Philadelphia: Industrial Research Unit, The Wharton School, University of Pennsylvania, 1977).

firmative action at AT&T, the following model was constructed. We focus on the occupational classification of officials and managers; our results, however, will provide insights to the long-run problems that will be encountered in other job categories. In addition, we consider only the racial groups analyzed by Schneider.

Because our interviews noted an increasing emphasis either on a technical aptitude or a strong business background as prerequisites for success in management, we employ Schneider's projections for the supply of engineers and accountants in 1985. The supply of engineers is a proxy for the availability of technically trained professionals while that of accountants reflects the supply of professionals with business training.

Recent AT&T hiring practice has shown a breakdown of 45 percent of all new management hires having technical backgrounds and 55 percent nontechnical. If this composition is projected, then we would expect the long-run labor force to reflect this 45 percent technical and 55 percent nontechnical (business) split.[4] Using the logic of statistical parity, we would expect that this 45–55 division would be reflected in each race-sex group. Were this not the case, statistical parity would necessitate the conclusion that job discrimination existed.

Given the above, we are ready to employ the Schneider analysis. Table VI-2 gives Schneider's projections on the percentage composition of the supply of engineers and accountants in 1985. These percentage figures are taken relative to a labor force composed only of the above-listed four racial groups; if Hispanics and other minorities were included, the figures would be lowered slightly.

For example, Schneider computed the percentage representation for white females in engineering by taking the ratio of white females in engineering to all whites and blacks in engineering. If we were to expand the denominator by including Hispanics and other minorities in engineering, the percentage figure computed would decline. As is seen below, this adds even greater strength to our conclusions.

Table VI-2 presents graphically a serious potential constraint that will be confronted by any major employer seeking to implement affirmative action. Even with programs to increase minority group and white female participation in engineering and business curricula, the labor force in 1985 in these professions will still be overwhelmingly dominated by white males.

If AT&T were to follow the logic of statistical parity, then the

---

4 "EEO Reference Binder," p. 1.

TABLE VI-2

*Projected Percentage Composition of the United States
by Race and Sex, Engineering and Accounting Labor Force, 1985*

Race–Sex Group	Engineering	Accounting
White Males	96.69	83.11
White Females	1.56	12.06
Black Males	1.71	3.95
Black Females	0.04	0.88

Source: Schneider, *Availability of Minorities and Women,* pp. 41, 89.

technical and nontechnical components of its managerial labor force in 1985 would have a race-sex composition given by Table VI-2. Thus, in the case of technically trained managers, statistical parity would dictate that 96.7 percent of them would be white males, 1.6 percent white females, 1.7 percent black males, and 0.04 percent black females. Similar results would also hold for nontechnical managers using the percentage breakdown of accountants given in the same table.

Using the 45–55 split, we can derive the ultimate supply of workers available for employment at AT&T if the company were to achieve statistical parity in its labor force by 1985. Thus, in the case of white females, we would expect to see this race-sex group accounting for 7.3 percent of all managerial positions. This figure is obtained in the following way:

$$0.45\,(1.6) + 0.55\,(12.1) = 7.3 \text{ percent}$$

Similar computations can be carried out for the remaining race-sex groups. The results are presented in the left-hand column of Table VI-3; the right column of this table gives the ultimate goal, or target percentage, of the AT&T labor force for each race-sex group.[5]

In spite of the largest affirmative action program pursued to date, and this by the largest private sector firm, ultimate goals will not be realized in any category by 1985. The projected percentages for the protected group members listed in Table VI-3 actually overstate the true figure because of the absence of Hispanics and other minorities from the analysis. The discrepancy between projected percentages and ultimate goals is even greater for white females and blacks.

The AT&T Pool

The above model implicitly assumes that technical and accounting professionals are uniformly distributed among all com-

---

[5] *Ibid.,* Section F.

TABLE VI-3
*AT&T, Projected Composition of Labor Force
by Race and Sex, Officials and Managers, 1985*

Race–Sex Group	Projected Percentage	Ultimate Goal
White Males	89.2	51.5
White Females	7.3	30.8
Black Males	2.9	6.4
Black Females	0.5	4.9

Source: Derived from AT&T projections and Schneider, *Availability of Minorities and Women.*

panies hiring workers. A more instructive analysis would be to determine the total supply of technical and business professionals and inquire whether there will be a sufficient pool from which AT&T can choose and still meet its goals.

We begin by noting that the average yearly growth in the managerial labor force in the Bell System was 3.09 percent from 1973 to 1979. This trend, projected to 1985, yields a total managerial labor force of 236,839. (See Appendix VI-B for a derivation of this figure.) Using the ultimate goals previously given we can determine the required employment mix for our four race-sex groups.

In addition to conducting an analysis of the projected percentage composition of the labor force, Dr. Schneider also projected total supplies of professionals in engineering, accounting, and general business. These projections were later revised by the Industrial Research Unit as part of an internal study. The revision employed updated figures not available at the time of the initial analysis. Although there is a negligible difference between the initial Schneider projections and the more recent estimates, the latter are presented in Table VI-4.

Using the above and combining the totals for accounting and general business in the nontechnical category, we can proceed with our analysis. We again employ the 45–55 split between technical and nontechnical workers. Table VI-5 presents our results.

Although Table VI-5 shows that there will be enough protected group workers to meet AT&T's long-run targets, it does not tell the whole story. Other firms will also be competing for these same workers. Assume, for simplicity, that these firms also maintain the 45–55 split. Given this, Table VI-6 shows the percentage of total supply that AT&T must capture to achieve its ultimate goals by 1985. In each case, this percentage is computed by taking the ratio of AT&T demand to total labor supply as given in Table VI-5.

Table VI-6 still shows some long-run difficulties for the implementation of affirmative action, even though AT&T is the

TABLE VI-4

Projected Percentage Composition of United States
by Race and Sex, Professional Labor Force, 1985

Race–Sex Group	Engineering	Accounting	General Business
White Males	1,299,970	509,469	2,083,543
White Females	20,925	73,929	233,811
Black Males	22,918	24,218	171,366
Black Females	568	5,408	33,448

Source: Schneider, *Availability of Minorities and Women*, pp. 41, 89, and 118. (Data revised to include previously unavailable material; identical methodology utilized.)

TABLE VI-5

Projected Labor Force Demand and Supply by Race and Sex
Officials and Managers, 1985

Race–Sex Group	Demand	Supply
White Males	121,972	2,011,143
White Females	72,946	178,673
Black Males	15,158	117,884
Black Females	11,605	21,626

Source: Derived from AT&T projections and Schneider, *Availability of Minorities and Women.*

TABLE VI-6

Percentage of Available Supply in the United States
Needed to Achieve Company Ultimate Goals by 1985

Race–Sex Group	Percent
White Males	6.1
White Females	40.8
Black Males	12.9
Black Females	53.7

Source: Derived from AT&T projections and Schneider, *Availability of Minorities and Women.*

largest employer in the country. To achieve its ultimate goals, AT&T would have to garner more than half of the qualified black females in the United States by 1985. The figure for white females exceeds 40 percent of the total qualified labor force. The recruiting costs alone would be staggering. The increased salaries needed to bid these professionals away from other employers also compounds AT&T's problems.

To understand fully the magnitude of this problem, we must situate AT&T in the total labor market for engineers. In 1976 (the latest year for which figures are available), the communications industry, of which AT&T is the dominant firm, employed approximately 10.3 percent of all engineers in the United States.[6] To be able to achieve the gains needed by 1985, this proportion must be expanded significantly in the case of protected group members. It is highly doubtful that AT&T will be able to accomplish this, especially in view of the resurgence of the aerospace industry, which is the country's largest industry employer of engineers and scientists, and the increasing demands for engineers resulting from the energy crisis and environmental problems.[7]

The above analysis deals solely in terms of the total labor supply. Quality differentials are nowhere mentioned. AT&T is interested in top quality management, and thus, in the case of white females, it must compete for a much larger percentage of the highly qualified portion of the total pool.

Prospects for black males, on the other hand, look fairly good. Only 12.8 percent of the available supply will be needed if AT&T is to attain its ultimate goal. Even allowing for problems with labor force quality, sufficient numbers of black males should be available for employment in the Bell System by 1985.

The authors grant the tenuous nature of predictions made six years into the future. There are strong assumptions that must be made to achieve our results. The assumptions, however, do not hide the basic fact that target fulfillment programs will confront a supply constraint that will ultimately affect the ability of firms to alter significantly the composition of their labor force.

In fact, this process has already occurred at AT&T, at least for minorities. In 1976, the latest year for which data are available, minority group males with technical backgrounds hired into management declined by 10.4 percent. The hiring of minority group females with this same background declined by 2.1 percent.[8] Based upon our analysis, this demand trend should continue well into the future as AT&T and other firms compete for the small supply of qualified minority applicants.

CONCLUSION

We have examined the long-run trends in labor supply and demand at AT&T. Our analysis has shown an increasing demand

---

[6] U.S., Department of Labor, Bureau of Labor Statistics, *Occupational Outlook Handbook 1978–1979*, Bulletin No. 1955 (Washington, D.C.: U.S. Government Printing Office, 1978), p. 342.

[7] *Ibid.*

[8] "EEO Reference Binder," Section XIV.

for technically trained workers at all levels. In addition, we have seen a geographic concentration of employment opportunities in the Southwest and West. Protected group workers must thus be more mobile in the future if they wish to seek employment at the Bell System.

Abstracting from the problem of geographic concentration, we considered the question of the supply of qualified protected group workers to fill the openings resulting from AT&T's affirmative action efforts. Focusing on management through the use of a simulation model developed by Dr. Stephen Schneider, we noted potential long-run problems in the availability of white and black females.

Such supply shortages cast serious doubts on the long-run viability of the consent decree program. More to the point, what is the time horizon for affirmative action? If, as seems likely in the case of black and white females, ultimate goals have not been reached by 1985, do we blindly push on? Or do we reassess our programs and accept the fact that drastic changes in the racial and sex composition of the work force are not easily achieved even by the enforcement of quotas?

Appendix VI-A

THE AVAILABILITY SIMULATION

We present here the briefest outline of Dr. Schneider's model.[1] The interested reader wishing to pursue this further is referred to chapter II of Schneider's work for a full discussion.

The labor supply process, as simulated by Schneider, relies on the following equation:

$$(UE+E)_{N+1} = (UE+E)_N + (TP+OC+NLF+I)_{N \rightarrow N+1}$$
$$- (D+R+T+OL)_{N \rightarrow N+1}$$

Where:

E   = Employment
UE   = Unemployment
TP   = Entrants to the labor force from training programs
OC   = Entrants from other occupations
NLF   = Entrants from outside the labor force
I   = Immigrants
D   = Deaths
R   = Retirements
T   = Transfers
OL   = Other losses (e.g., emigrants)

In other words, the equation states that the total labor supply at time $N + 1$ is the sum of three separate factors: those in the profession at time N (the first bracketed term) and new entrants between period $N + 1$ and N (the second bracketed term) less all those who have left the labor force between period $N + 1$ and period N (the third bracketed term).

Demographic data were simulated on the computer using this equation of the labor supply process yielding the results listed in Tables V-3 and V-5.

---

[1] Stephen A. Schneider, *The Availability of Minorities and Women for Professional and Managerial Positions 1970–1985,* Manpower and Human Resources Studies No. 7 (Philadelphia: Industrial Research Unit, The Wharton School, University of Pennsylvania, 1977).

Appendix VI-B

DERIVATION OF THE 1985 MANAGEMENT LABOR FORCE

We have seen in Chapter II that total officials and managers employed in the Bell System were 164,438 in 1973 and 191,436 on January 17, 1979. If we assume a constant growth rate of employment, λ, during these years, we obtain:

$$614,438 \, (1 + \lambda)^{1978-1973} = 191,436$$
$$(1 + \lambda)^5 = 1.164$$
$$\lambda = 3.09 \text{ percent}$$

If this growth rate persists until 1985, we obtain a demand for officials and managers of the following magnitude:

$$164,438 \, (1.0309)^{1985-1973} = 164,438 \, (1.0309)^{12} = 236,839$$

Applying the 45–55 breakdown yields the figures given in chapter VI.

CHAPTER VII

An Overall Evaluation

We have examined at the national and regional levels the changes in the race-sex composition of the AT&T labor force that have occurred since 1973. We have also discussed the possible effects on operational performance and the cost implications of the consent decree. In this section, we assess the overall results of the program and their implications for the major firms in American industry.

We begin by analyzing the government's strategy in bringing charges against AT&T. Perhaps more significantly, we examine the key idea that not only formed the foundation of the government's argument against AT&T but that also underlies the program eventually implemented—statistical parity of the labor force. Our previous chapters have shown that affirmative action at AT&T has succeeded in job classifications where no attempt has been made to alter the traditional job expectations of American workers. When the opposite has occurred (females in outside crafts, male secretaries), serious problems have been encountered. Because nontraditional employment reflects a commitment to statistical parity, a careful assessment of the AT&T experience must include a reexamination of this concept.

THE RATIONALE OF THE EEOC

Traditional economic theory can lead to the conclusion that if discrimination in labor markets is to occur, it will most probably be observed in regulated industries. Suppose, for example, that society decides to pay a group of workers inordinately low wages given their job skills. Then, theoretically, unregulated firms can be expected to attempt to hire more of these workers in order to increase their profits.

Regulated firms, such as electric utilities and AT&T, according to these theoreticians, have no such incentive to employ this group because their profits are set by law. There is thus no opportunity to augment profits by hiring a disadvantaged group. Reasoning such as the above has been applied to the AT&T case.

Research by several economists has indicated that firms which are sheltered from competition tend to discriminate more than firms which are subject to the full force of competition. Companies which are sheltered from competition either because of their large size relative to the market or because they are in a field where regulation takes the place of competition seem to have the opportunity to ignore sources of black and female labor with impunity.[1]

In fact, however, the basis of corporate racial policies is far more complicated and sophisticated than this simplistic analysis indicates. As the Studies of Negro Employment, published by the Wharton School's Industrial Research Unit,[2] clearly demonstrates by factual, rather than theoretical, analysis, many factors have determined the racial composition of an industry's work force: the demand for labor, the nature of the work, the time and nature of the industry's development, the mores of the community, the degree of consumer orientation, the concern of the industry or company for its image, community crises, the nature of union organization, the impact of technology, the industry's location, the role of government, and managerial action and policy.[3]

Most of these criteria played a role in the development of AT&T's racial employment and employment policies, as set forth in Professor Anderson's monograph in the Studies of Negro Employment series.[4] For example, blacks made their greatest initial gains in the Bell System during World War II when the demand for labor was high and government policy to employ minorities was initiated. Women were not employed for AT&T's inside craft categories because the corporation froze a historical pattern of the time and nature of the period when the jobs were created. AT&T always has had a concern for its image and has a strong consumer market orientation; therefore, over the years, its employment policies have generally reflected *current* mores and attitudes, although sometimes they fell behind in some respects (as in inside crafts) but never got too far out of line with public taste. Of great

---

[1] Barbara R. Bergmann and Jill Gordon King, "Diagnosing Discrimination," in *Equal Employment Opportunity and the AT&T Case*, ed. Phyllis A. Wallace (Cambridge, Mass.: MIT Press, 1976), p. 49.

[2] A full list of the eight volumes in this series and the thirty-one monographs in the Racial Policies of American Industries studies are found on the back pages, below.

[3] Herbert R. Northrup et al., *Negro Employment in Basic Industry*, Studies of Negro Employment, Vol. I (Philadelphia: Industrial Research Unit, The Wharton School, University of Pennsylvania, 1970), pp. 3–4, 719–68.

[4] Bernard E. Anderson, *Negro Employment in Public Utilities*, Studies of Negro Employment, Vol. III (Philadelphia: Industrial Research Unit, The Wharton School, University of Pennsylvania, 1970).

importance, too, is the nature of the work—clean, pleasant, and reasonably prestigious. Prior to the enactment of the Civil Rights Act, minorities were concentrated in arduous, difficult, or unpleasant work and women in clerical or similar functions regardless of whether the industry was regulated or unregulated.

Of major importance in AT&T's employment policies has been the role of government. Anderson has pointed out that employment during the development of the modern utility was strongly influenced by politicians and ward leaders and that the racial and ethnic composition of the labor force reflected that of the area in which the utility operated.[5] Similarly, it has been noted:

> Regulated industries are of course regulated by politically appointed commissioners, so that while their hiring policies have fewer economic constraints . . . they are even more subject to political constraints. This means that while there is likely to be more racial discrimination in a regulated industry than in an unregulated industry during periods when there is no great public outcry against discrimination, the regulated industries would be forced to make a more sudden about face on discrimination than the unregulated industries when political forces attack discrimination.[6]

It is precisely this logic that forms the rationale for the EEO regulators' strategy against AT&T. Because the telephone industry is highly regulated, the EEOC was able to use leverage against AT&T to obtain the necessary concessions on affirmative action by intruding on a regulatory matter—a petition for a rate increase on long distance phone calls. Firms such as General Electric and those in the steel industry, which signed consent decrees after AT&T pioneered in this respect, operate in a relatively freer regulatory climate. Choosing them as the initial object of litigation in the EEO area may well not have produced the results obtained by bringing charges against AT&T.

Given the regulatory nature of the industrial environment and also its size, AT&T was the logical target for the EEOC. By using the influence of its regulatory power, the government was able to exert sufficient leverage that it would not have had with an unregulated private sector firm and induce the nation's largest private sector employer to adopt a path-breaking affirmative action program.

Having made AT&T fall, the government was able to use this as heavy artillery against other large private sector firms. The

---

[5] *Ibid.*, pp. 68–72.

[6] Thomas Sowell, *Race and Economics* (New York: David McKay Company, Inc., 1975), p. 167.

government, in effect, sent "signals" to American industry as a result of the AT&T experience to convince major firms that the time for affirmative action had come. Since then companies such as General Electric, Bank of America, United Airlines, United States Steel, Bethlehem Steel, and many others have erected major programs to accelerate the hiring and promotion of protected groups. Those firms that do not have explicitly stated programs are also accutely aware of the need to increase protected worker visibility.

THE THEORY OF STATISTICAL PARITY

Once AT&T or another company is targeted by EEOC or other government enforcement agencies, pervasive discrimination may be alleged by resorting to the theory of statistical parity. Here we outline this approach as developed by one of its foremost exponents, Professor Barbara Bergmann, and then proceed to a critique of its underlying assumptions. We conclude that statistical parity, although being a straightforward concept to operationalize from a public policy perspective, has questionable applicability to the employee selection process. Furthermore, it is our contention that the failure to recognize the limits of this theory has contributed to some of the negative aspects of the AT&T experience under the consent decree, such as the problems encountered by female employment in outside crafts.

The Theory Explained

A cogent explanation of the theory of statistical parity and its applicability to affirmative action cases has been developed by Professor Bergmann and Jill King.

> In order for information on employment composition to be meaningful, a comparison must be made with some benchmark. The benchmark must indicate on a realistic basis the fair share of each group in employment in a particular occupation. On what basis can such a "fair share" be computed? One principle with considerable appeal is that if for each occupation we can delimit the group in the labor force which is qualified for that occupation, then each race-sex group ... would eventually have approximately the same share in the jobs of that occupation as they would have in the qualified group. For example, if a job legitimately requires a college degree, and if Negro males constitute three percent of the group in the labor force with college degrees, then it seems reasonable, lacking information about other requirements, to say that Negro males should have three percent of jobs in that company of that particular type.[7]

---

[7] Bergmann and King, "Diagnosing Discrimination," p. 50.

Under what conditions will the above hold? What are the implicit assumptions underlying the Bergmann approach? Simply put, statistical parity is a derivative of the process of random selection. For example, suppose we wanted to determine how many voters will cast their ballots for a certain Republican candidate in the next presidential election. We could accomplish this in one of two ways: (1) We could personally contact each voter in the nation and ask whether he or she will vote for the Republican candidate, or (2) We could select a sample that approximates the characteristics of the electorate and then canvass this smaller group for their electoral preferences. Clearly the cost of alternative (1) is prohibitive; therefore, survey organizations have recourse to the latter approach.

One method of achieving a sample that approximates the underlying electorate is the technique known as random sampling.[8] Random sampling is analogous to selecting balls from an urn. For example, suppose a jar is filled with fifty balls—twenty black, ten white, ten red, five green, and 5 blue. The percentage composition of the balls in the container is thus 40 percent black, 20 percent white, 20 percent red, 10 percent green, and 10 percent blue.

If we were to close our eyes and simply pick five balls from this jar we would find that, on average, the colors of the balls selected would approximate the percentage composition outlined above. That is, the sample of five balls should reflect the same breakdown by color as that of the underlying population of fifty balls. In short, random selection will lead to an approximate correspondence between the sample drawn and the population. It is important to note that in this procedure the composition of the underlying population, i.e., the balls in the urn, must remain the same throughout the selection process.

When this method is applied to the employee selection process, we have the concept of statistical parity. Instead of an urn of balls from which we will choose a sample we have a qualified employee pool from which we will choose our labor force. This employment pool is then broken down by race and sex.

Nondiscriminatory employment practices are thus analogous to the blindfolded selection of balls from an urn. Those in charge of hiring workers simply close their eyes and randomly choose their labor force from the underlying employment pool. As a result, the race and sex composition of the company's labor force should ap-

---

[8] For a full discussion of the theory of random selection, see W. G. Cochran, *Sampling Techniques* (New York: John Wiley and Sons, 1977).

proximate that of the pool from which it is drawn.

Nondiscriminatory hiring (random selection) will lead, given the assumption of a constant distribution of the underlying employment pool, to a labor force whose composition by race and sex is a mirror image of that of the larger pool. Conversely, if a company's labor force does not reflect this parity, then it must have practiced nonrandom selection. Nonrandom selection in this context is interpreted as discriminatory hiring practices.

> In the New Jersey Bell Telephone Company, for example, 4.4 percent of the telephone craftsmen were black . . . . [Yet] for New Jersey Bell, black males constituted 8.0 percent of males eligible for telephone crafts jobs. On this basis, New Jersey Bell had only 55 percent of the black male telephone craftsmen it would have had in the absence of discrimination against black males as against white males.[9]

A CRITICAL EVALUATION OF STATISTICAL PARITY

Two main criticisms can be invoked against the theory of statistical parity. The first involves the definition of the appropriate employment pool from which the company's labor force is selected. The second criticism concerns the equation of nondiscriminatory hiring practices with the theory of random selection. In other words, is the decision to employ an individual really analogous to the blindfolded selection of balls from an urn? We consider each of these points in turn.

Definition of the Underlying Labor Pool

Assume for this section that a company follows random selection in its hiring practices. It is still possible for its labor force not to demonstrate statistical parity. This will occur whenever the underlying labor pool from which the company selects its employees differs from that used by the government in its analysis of racial discrimination.

Consider the definition of the underlying labor pool as propounded by Bergmann and Krause:

> One principle with considerable appeal is that if for each occupation we can delimit the group in the labor force which is "qualified" for that occupation, then Negroes eventually should have the same share in the jobs of that occupation as they have in the qualified group. In the computations made for entire industries, we have adopted a very simple definition of qualification based on years of schooling completed. . . .
>
> In establishing this "qualification" criterion we obviously are

---

[9] Bergmann and King, "Diagnosing Discrimination," p. 51.

ignoring other dimensions of the problem: quality of education, experience, and other relevant personal characteristics.[10]

These "other dimensions," specifically experience and quality of education, not to mention the quality of the worker and his motivation level, are extremely important in delimiting the appropriate labor pool for a company. In our interviews with operating company officials throughout the country, differences in the quality of education received for a given amount of total schooling were continually noted.

Differences in experience levels also exist for the same total level of schooling. This was especially noticeable in outside crafts where officials referred to it as a prime cause of accident rate differentials between males and females.

It is evident, then, that simply relying on years of schooling will ignore some extremely important determinants involved in the hiring process. In all fairness to Bergmann and Krause, they acknowledge that their approach is designed "to contribute to a broad-brush picture" of discrimination.[11] The problem, however, remains. Once quality and experience differentials are acknowledged, the true underlying employment pool can differ drastically from an artificial pool based solely on years of education.

In point of fact, then, a company may actually be practicing nondiscriminatory hiring from an employment pool that takes into account these differences and yet still be accused of biases in its practices when government agencies employ for purposes of comparison a labor pool based solely on years of education. Much further work remains to be done in this area if the theory of statistical parity is to be applied in a meaningful way in EEO judgments.

Other problems still remain in defining the underlying labor pool even after we take into account differences in quality and experience. Primary among these are regional mobility and ethnic differences with respect to attitudes toward different occupations.

For example, married women with families tend to be less geographically mobile than males. To the extent that employment at a company involves long commuting distances or extensive travel, the use of educational level as the sole criterion for defining the labor pool ignores an extremely important dimension of the

---

[10] Barbara Bergmann and William Krause, "Evaluating and Forecasting Progress in Racial Integration of Employment," *Industrial and Labor Relations Review*, Vol. 25, No. 3 (April 1972), pp. 401–02.

[11] *Ibid.*

problem. The same holds true for minority group members and other low-income recipients. To the extent that a company's business opportunities shift to affluent suburban areas, residents who remain behind in central cities may experience difficulties in commuting which will eliminate them from the relevant employment pool.

Intervening employment opportunities also play a major factor. Theoretical economists and equal employment administrators alike tend too often to regard city areas as a single labor market. Not only do commuting routes and tastes tend to divide up such markets but so do intervening opportunity with the shorter commute. A company located across a city from areas of black population concentration may therefore find that it is extremely difficult to recruit blacks who may in a real sense be in a different labor market area from this perspective employer.

Consider also the case of ethnic differences in work attitudes. Our interviews noted a reluctance of young Irish Catholic women to accept employment in outside craft positions. This reluctance effectively eliminates them from the relevant employment pool, something not taken into account in a criterion based solely on years of education. Other examples of this form of behavior were noted among Hispanics and Indians in particular.

In short, the use of census data quantifying educational levels as a means of defining the relevant employment pool presents a distorted view of the true underlying labor force. Such a broad definition ignores the various factors noted above and greatly exaggerates the supply of qualified protected workers available for employment. In all fairness to American industry, more work must be done in defining the "truly qualified" employment pool before the concept of statistical parity can be meaningfully applied as a method for analyzing race and sex discrimination.

Constancy of Labor Pool

One last difficulty remains: the assumption of a constant composition of the employment pool. Random selection will lead to statistical parity only when the underlying employment pool remains constant over time. The analogy that we previously introduced of drawing balls from an urn is appropriate here. If we were continually to alter the composition of balls in the urn, we would find that repeated drawings of balls would fail to produce proportions that would, on average, approximate the true distribution, because this distribution would be continually changing. The process would be equivalent to shooting at a moving target that never stays still long enough to be hit.

What causes the underlying labor force to change? Regional population shifts, changing labor force participation, and increases in years of schooling, especially among minorities and women, are of primary importance here. Consider, for example, the case of black males. One reason why they may be underrepresented in management in terms of statistical parity is that the bulk of managerial hiring may have taken place prior to the surge in black enrollment in colleges. A discrimination criterion that looks at current levels of education and then makes judgments concerning the past employment practices of a company will be inappropriate in a situation of the type just described.

Recent changes in female labor force participation is another factor. The amazing jump in recent years of women working and looking for work has meant a substantially larger pool of females from which employers can choose. This, in turn, means much more competition for minorities as well as for white males.

In summary, then, statistical parity, although appearing on face value to be a readily applicable concept in judging employment discrimination, is actually rather difficult to operationalize once its underlying assumptions are seriously considered. Quality differences, experience levels, commuting distances, intervening opportunity, and changes in the composition of the labor force are ignored in this approach. Questions of this sort must be satisfactorily resolved before the theory can be meaningfully applied. Until such is the case, we shall continue to experience the difficulties previously noted in nontraditional employment.

Does Random Selection Accurately Describe the Employment Decision?

The above discussion assumed that the decision to employ an individual was analogous to choosing balls randomly from an urn. We must now consider whether such an analogy holds. Do companies randomly select workers from an underlying labor pool or are other factors involved? Moreover, if random selection is not used can we truly claim that the employer is discriminating?

Actually, as we have already noted, a company's employment policies may depend on many factors, not the least of which is a much finer analysis of competency that government, unfamiliar with productive needs, can make. None of these decisions may constitute discrimination, but they certainly would not adhere to any random selection theory or confirm its result.

In addition, there are other types of nonrandom selection that are established in law. The preferential treatment of veterans, older workers, or handicapped persons are the prime examples, as discussed below. Thus, there are legal constraints that inhibit random selection, too. In short, there are legal barriers as well as legitimate employment goals that cast serious doubt on the applicability of a random selection process to the decision to hire an individual worker.

BACK PAY

Another interesting feature of the consent decree has been the introduction of the concept of back pay resulting from the presumed effects of past discrimination. To date the company has paid out approximately $18 million to alleged victims of prior substandard wages. In addition, AT&T has given pay increases to over 72,000 employees at a yearly annual cost of $53 million.

The purpose of back pay is twofold: it builds up support for the enforcement agency among protected groups and it serves notice on potential violators, or even litigants, that failure to expand employment opportunities can be costly. The second point is obvious; the first is equally significant to the agency involved and to its bureaucracy, which is usually looking for support for greater funding and enlarged staff.

In some cases, the cash penalties have been earmarked for training and development of protected groups. Undoubtedly, such awards or settlements have encouraged otherwise reluctant employers to redouble their efforts affirmatively to employ and to advance protected groups. In such cases, the concept of back pay or other financial awards or penalties can be defended as serving the purpose of Title VII of the Civil Rights Act.

On the other hand, the concentration of the civil rights agencies on securing back pay or financial awards to protected groups, which is apparent to any company charged by them, has a number of shortcomings. In the first place, back pay, while pleasant for the recipient, does not provide in itself for improvement in the job hierarchy. A person may receive a monetary award and still never better himself or learn to be qualified to better himself. The civil rights agency receives good publicity for winning the awards, but it may not have accomplished its statutory purpose—better integration of the work force—because of the staff's concentration on employer financial penalties.

Financial awards are also frequently given, as at AT&T, regardless of whether the individual is deserving. Thus a person who never had any interest in promotion, or whose qualifications are meager at best, can receive an award as well as can a thoroughly qualified person who was denied a job because of his race. This broad-brush approach, of course, is consistent with a belief that all protected groups are aggrieved. Yet it does seem inconsistent with public policy not to differentiate on the basis of actual individual experience.

Finally, large financial awards encourage litigation. Frequently, lawyers' fees depend on a successful award and court-awarded fees. To the extent that this system encourages the availability of able counsel to those who need lawyers but would otherwise not be able to afford them, it can certainly be defended as a forward step. On the other hand, the extent that it encourages protracted and unnecessary litigation, which may well be the situation, is both unfortunate and of tangential assistance at best to victims of discrimination.

CONFLICTS AMONG GOVERNMENT OBJECTIVES AND AGENCIES

Today, most Americans are in one or more protected groups. Besides all women and minorities, those protected include employees over forty-five years of age; the handicapped; veterans; and, in a few cases, sexual deviants. For most of these groups, both state and federal laws exist and sometimes municipal ones as well.

Obviously, the objectives of some of these laws tend to be in fundamental conflict with the objectives of others. For example, because most veterans are males, laws favoring their employment place barriers in the way of females. Likewise, because most Vietnam-era veterans are likely to be both male and under forty-five years of age for some time, laws favoring them discriminate against both females and older workers, and of course, vice-versa. When Congress abolished compulsory retirement at sixty-five years of age, it favored older workers at the expense of younger ones. In addition, because a major portion of older workers in better positions are likely to be white males, Congress in effect has slowed down the potential advancement of minorities and females who are upward bound but newer in terms of opportunities for advancement.

In the AT&T case, we have shown that women and minorities have profited in a disparate manner because it is not possible to satisfy requirements for one group without causing additional competition or barriers for another. Because females, in contrast to minorities, frequently come from well-endowed, middle-class families, and are well-educated, and are at least as ambitious and motivated, they did very well under the consent decree in the managerial positions. Thus the presence of very competent females and their upgrading has added further obstacles to minority advancement.

Table VII-1 summarizes the relative success in filling openings of white women and black men and women during 1973, the first year of the consent decree, and the period January 1, 1978 to mid-January 1979, when the consent decree terminated, using as illustrations four key occupational groups—management, sales workers, inside crafts, and outside crafts. In management, the number of black males filling openings was 1,036 (1,402 less 366) greater the last year than the first one. Black female placements increased by 1,245. White females, however, filled 5,091 more openings during the last year than during the first, more than double the gains of black males and females combined.

The data for the other positions yield similar results. Both in absolute and percentage gains, white females were the principal gainers. What this means for now and for the future is continued increasing competition for minorities who must compete not only against white males but against white females as well. Moreover, white females are, like minorities, a protected group and thus have affirmative action support for special treatment. This, plus their superior backgrounds and education, is likely to continue to push women ahead and to make minorities lagging gainers despite the belief of many that minority employment is the far greater social problem.

These results are not in conflict with the key objective of the government in the AT&T case, which was parity employment even if that was at the expense of more jobs for a protected group. We would argue, however, that the great social problem of our time is minority integration. We also support equal opportunity for females. But by setting quotas for females, the government may well have set back minorities who aspire to better jobs.

Parity employment as the key government objective, even at the expense of more jobs for protected groups, is apparent also in specific quotas. There is no other way to explain a quota for white males in the clerical function. Here the effect was to reduce female employment, not to expand it. Such an objective, which we believe to be questionable at best, discriminates against those females who

TABLE VII-1
AT&T, Job Openings Filled by Blacks and White Females
Four Occupational Groups, 1973 and 1978

| | Black Males | | | | Black Females | | | | White Females | | | |
| | 1973 | | 1978 | | 1973 | | 1978 | | 1973 | | 1978 | |
Occupational Group	Number	Percent	Number	Percent	Number	Percent	Number	Percent	Number	Percent	Number	Percent
Management	366	2.3	1,402	4.9	477	2.9	1,722	6.0	5,571	34.4	10,662	37.4
Sales Workers	66	4.2	213	7.2	90	5.7	283	9.6	687	43.6	1,120	37.9
Outside Crafts	2,027	11.0	1,456	8.4	45	0.2	467	2.7	678	3.7	3,117	18.1
Inside Crafts	653	5.4	399	5.0	508	4.2	760	9.5	4,021	32.9	3,588	44.8

Source: The Company.
Note: 1978 data run through January 15, 1979.

135

desire traditional employment. Of course, this does not mean that we object to males seeking employment in this function. What is objectionable is denying competent females an opportunity to work as clericals while requiring males to take training as secretaries in order to fulfill an artificially contrived quota.

Something of the same mentality went into the quota for females in outside crafts. As we have pointed out, this quota had no scientific basis but was contrived by dividing the then current total labor force participation ratio of women by one-half. The result was a massive expenditure by the company for training and turnover and extraordinary frustration on the part of numerous women who found after great effort and much time that they either lacked qualifications or found the work distasteful. Meanwhile, qualified men were denied such jobs and were thereby discriminated against in order to satisfy the EEO regulators' goal of parity employment.

The insistance on an artificially high quota for female outside craft workers also emphasizes another conflict of government policy. Despite great emphasis on training and safety, including allowing personnel to train at an individual pace, the accident rate for females in these jobs has been alarming and substantially higher than for males. Thus, to achieve a contrived quota dedicated to a parity concept without any factual basis, one branch of the government ignored the implications of its action for another aspect of public policy as expressed in the Occupational Safety and Health Act.

The problem of conflict among regulators, agencies, and statutory policies is well illustrated by the experience of AT&T under the consent decree but is not unique. For example, chemical companies may be technically violating Title VII of the Civil Rights Act by removing childbearing-age women from employment in plant areas where chemicals may adversely affect a fetus; affirmative action plans conflict with seniority provisions negotiated between management and unions pursuant to the National Labor Relations (Taft-Hartley) Act; and there are the conflicts involving different protected groups as already noted. AT&T was able to move in one direction under the umbrella of the consent decree. What its experience illustrates is, first, that a consent decree so designed results nevertheless in some significantly questionable policies and results; and second, that the myriad of rules, regulations, and policy directions to which industry is now subject in the social area results in gains toward one objective but often at the expense of serious losses in others. Obviously, a better and less simplistic approach would consider, for example, safety before an artificial quota is pulled out of the air; or the relative urgency of minority and female upgrading before prescribing targets; or the wisdom of refusing jobs to qualified females as clericals while training males for the jobs.

EFFECTIVENESS OF THE DECREE

We have examined the government's affirmative action strategy having noted the decision to use a large, vulnerable company as a lever with which to force other firms to implement preferential hiring and promotion plans. Furthermore, we have noted some of the costs imposed on AT&T (and presumably potentially on other large corporations) and the implications thereof that emanated from the consent decree—back pay, training expenses, and increased accidents being conspicuous examples.

We must now inquire what has been received for these costs. Results should always be judged relative to some standard or objective. In what follows we postulate some reasonable objectives for an affirmative action program and then evaluate the progress made toward these goals at AT&T.

Increased Utilization

An affirmative action program should lead to increasing utilization of protected groups. In terms of numbers, this certainly occurred for all minority groups. For females, however, the percentage in the Bell System fell slightly. Moreover, as we shall see below, the decline in white female representation was isolated among certain educational and skill levels.

Expanded Opportunity for All

An affirmative action program should provide expanded employment opportunities for all workers within a given protected group. It should not result in expanded opportunities for one segment of a protected group while increasing discrimination for another segment of the same group. That would seem to run at cross-purposes to the main purpose of equal opportunity legislation. Yet this is exactly what has happened at AT&T where affirmative action has been based on the concept of statistical parity. For example, white female opportunities increased in management and outside craft positions, but they declined in clerical and phone operator use. There is thus no question that the consent decree has been extremely beneficial to the college-educated, technically trained white females. Their numbers in management have increased dramatically since 1973.

This, however, is small consolation to the white woman who has just successfully completed a secretarial course at high school and who wants to work in the area in which she is trained. She could seek a job in outside crafts but may not be qualified, may fear such work, or may come from a cultural background that makes such a job unthinkable. Why should she be denied opportunity in order to expand the number of males as clericals or operators?

The same reasoning can be applied to other race-sex groups. Are affirmative action programs, based on the concept of statistical parity, really helping the right individuals? College-educated, technically trained individuals of any race and sex are in short supply. Opportunities are relatively numerous for such people. Do college-educated blacks, Hispanics, and females really need a government program to insure them a plethora of opportunities? Yet in the program at AT&T, the government has assisted the college-trained much more than the more disadvantaged.

Other Benefits and Costs

AT&T has benefited as well as suffered costs under the decree. A primary one for the company has been an improvement in the utilization of female talent. This has been most apparent in management and inside craft work. After interviewing AT&T officials throughout the country, one must ask why this talent was not properly employed before. Whatever the answer the fact remains that the consent decree provided the stimulus for Bell System operating companies to reap benefits from a highly educated and motivated female labor force.

Second, AT&T has also greatly expanded opportunities for minorities in all job classes. This affords the company a greater labor market source. In addition, through their recruiting efforts, operating companies have made minority group members aware of these opportunities. The Bell System's stress on advancement possibilities open to those with the proper training and background has been a stimulus for minority group educational and professional advancement.

A third benefit is the increased emphasis on human resource management within the Bell System. Promotion paths have been more clearly delineated. The advancement process has been centralized in the personnel office leading to larger numbers of workers competing for a given advancement. The quality of those receiving promotions has increased.

These benefits, however, have not been costless, and a large burden of this cost has been borne by AT&T's white male employees. Our analysis has shown that minority and female gains have come at the expense of white males. In addition to the obvious loss of morale that this has caused, one can only speculate as to the long-run implications for the Bell System resulting from the reduction in opportunities for the primary component of the American labor force.

Another important cost of the decree has been the substitution of "basically qualified" for the merit system of "most qualified." In many cases, race and sex have become the primary determinant of advancement. Time-in-grade requirements for advancement have been waived when targets must be met, thereby depriving managers and supervisors of the broad base of experience needed to do their job. Again, the long-run implications of this have yet to be determined.

A special burden has also been placed on supervisors as a result of the AT&T affirmative action program. Deprived of much of their input into the employee advancement process, supervisors have struggled to adapt to the new environment of targets and quotas. This has been compounded by the use of the EEO counsellors, whom the supervisors regard as a subversion of the chain of command. In addition, extra burdens for productivity increases have been placed on supervisors as the communications industry becomes more competitive. This stress on obtaining increased output from a "basically qualified" labor force has compounded the problems of supervisors.

We have noted other costs—back pay, more extensive training, and higher accident rates—which need not again be reemphasized. It is well, however, to mention again that the emphasis on female advancement under the decree seems certain to place additional burdens in the future on minority job opportunities.

FINAL COMMENT

The individual observer must evaluate for himself whether benefits of the AT&T decree were worth the costs. It is likely that they were, given the nation's commitment and need for better integration of the work force. We believe, however, that the costs could have been lower if the government regulators were less committed to parity employment and more committed to increased employment opportunities. We have found the theory of statistical parity ill-conceived and inapplicable as a measure of non-discrimination. We have further shown by our analysis that emphasis on statistical parity results in serious costs. One could therefore hope that government administrators would emphasize equal employment instead of aiming for statistical results that ignore labor market realities.

Unfortunately, this is not likely to be the case. The decision of the United States Supreme Court in *United Steelworkers v. Weber*[12] has been hailed by the EEOC as giving the green light to all affirmative action plans, including quota arrangements. In fact, however, the decision was a very narrow one, being confined to non-state action, voluntary plans outside the scope of Executive Order 11246. Furthermore, the Court's decision was predicated on the fact that the plan was not governmentally required, was enacted by private parties, and had as its purpose the elimination of manifest racial imbalance in traditionally segregated categories.[13] Whether, therefore, governmental EEO enforcement agencies hve been authorized to continue to concentrate on racial balance, which we believe can thwart equal opportunity, remains to be determined.

---

[12] ____ U.S. ____ (1979), 99 Sup.Ct. 2721, *rev'd*, 563 F.2d 216 (1978), *aff'd*, 415 F.Supp. 761 (1976).

[13] We are indebted to an analysis of the *Weber* decision by Douglas S. McDowell, Esq., of the Washington, D.C., firm, McGuiness and Williams, which was prepared for the Equal Employment Advisory Council.

Index

Racial Policies of American Industry Series

Order from: Kraus Reprint Co., Route 100, Millwood, New York 10546

STUDIES OF NEGRO EMPLOYMENT

Vol. I. *Negro Employment in Basic Industry: A Study of Racial Policies in Six Industries (Automobile, Aerospace, Steel, Rubber Tires, Petroleum, and Chemicals)*, by Herbert R. Northrup, Richard L. Rowan, et al. 1970. *

Vol. II. *Negro Employment in Finance: A Study of Racial Policies in Banking and Insurance*, by Armand J. Thieblot, Jr., and Linda Pickthorne Fletcher. 1970. *

Vol. III. *Negro Employment in Public Utilities: A Study of Racial Policies in the Electric Power, Gas, and Telephone Industries*, by Bernard E. Anderson. 1970. *

Vol. IV. *Negro Employment in Southern Industry: A Study of Racial Policies in the Paper, Lumber, Tobacco, Coal Mining, and Textile Industries*, by Herbert R. Northrup, Richard L. Rowan, et al. 1971. *

Vol. V. *Negro Employment in Land and Air Transport: A Study of Racial Policies in the Railroad, Airline, Trucking, and Urban Transit Industries*, by Herbert R. Northrup, Howard W. Risher, Jr., Richard D. Leone, and Philip W. Jeffress. 1971. $13.50

Vol. VI. *Negro Employment in Retail Trade: A Study of Racial Policies in the Department Store, Drugstore, and Supermarket Industries*, by Gordon F. Bloom, F. Marion Fletcher, and Charles R. Perry. 1972. *

Vol. VII. *Negro Employment in the Maritime Industries: A Study of Racial Policies in the Shipbuilding, Longshore, and Offshore Maritime Industries*, by Lester Rubin, William S. Swift, and Herbert R. Northrup. 1974. *

Vol. VIII. *Black and Other Minority Participation in the All-Volunteer Navy and Marine Corps*, by Herbert R. Northrup, Steven M. DiAntonio, John A. Brinker, and Dale F. Daniel. 1979. *

Order from the Industrial Research Unit
The Wharton School, University of Pennsylvania
Philadelphia, Pennsylvania 19104

*Order these books from University Microfilms, Inc., Attn: Books Editorial Department, 300 North Zeeb Road, Ann Arbor, Michigan 48106.

3417